D0949571

THE E-MYTH MANAGER

THE E-MYTH MANAGER

WHY MANAGEMENT DOESN'T WORK

—AND WHAT TO DO ABOUT IT

MICHAEL GERBER

HarperBusiness
A Division of HarperCollins*Publishers*

HarperCollins books may be purchased for educational, business, or sales promotional use. For information please write: Special Markets Department, HarperCollins Publishers, Inc., 10 East 53rd Street, New York, NY 10022.

FIRST EDITION

Designed by Alma Hochhauser Orenstein

Library of Congress Cataloging-in-Publication Data

Gerber, Michael E.
    The E-myth manager : why management doesn't work—and what to do about it / Michael Gerber.
        p.   cm.
    ISBN 0-88730-840-6
        1. Entrepreneurship.   2. Small business—management.
    3. Management.   I. Title.
    HD62.7.G457   1998   98-6531
    658—dc21

---

98 99 00 01 02 ❖/RRD 10 9 8 7 6 5 4 3 2

To Ilene, my wife, my partner, my love,
who would have thought?

CONTENTS

CONTENTS

ACKNOWLEDGMENTS

They say that behind every successful project is a host of committed people. In my case they are: my editor, Laureen Connelly Rowland, who not only carried me through this book, but at times seemed to lift me over her head; my extraordinary children, Shana, Kim, Hillary, Sam, and Alex, for all their love and patience; Jeff Gospe, Alex Alexander, and Janice Drescher, with whom I carried on extended and often intense conversations which sometimes bordered on the ridiculous, but also enabled each of us to turn unforeseen and surprising corners in our respective minds; The E-Myth Academy folks, past, present, and future, particularly Marilyn Geary, Joan Beane, Swati Sen, Katherine Ahlborn, April Gospe, and Vickie Norris, whose commitment, conviction, passion, and intelligence has, does, and will continue to see our clients over their at times seemingly impossible hurdles; our Certified E-Myth Consultants world-wide who have made, continue to make, and wish with all their hearts to make our mutual Vision possible; and our many thousands of E-Myth clients, who continue to persevere when perseverance is called for, to make their lives, and the lives of their people, truly and stunningly remarkable . . . thank you all; I couldn't have done any of this without you!

PREFACE

It has been more than ten years since my first book, *The E-Myth: Why Most Small Businesses Don't Work and What to Do About It*, was published. In that book, I described what I had learned over the ten previous years in our small business consulting firm, then the Michael Thomas Corporation, now The E-Myth Academy, about why small businesses fail to fulfill their potential. Why? The presumption—the entrepreneurial myth—is that most businesses are started by Entrepreneurs; the truth is that most businesses are started by Technicians suffering from an entrepreneurial seizure—the pie maker goes into the pie business; the mechanic opens an automotive repair business; the physician starts a medical practice. The Technician makes the fatal assumption that because he knows how to do the technical work of the business, he knows how to build a business that works. Unfortunately for him and for the business he creates, the opposite is true; and so most businesses fail, or if they don't fail outright, they fail to realize their potential.

More than two decades later, the lessons I have learned from our work with more than fifteen thousand small, medium-sized, and large—very, very large—organizations, provide me with an even deeper understanding of not only why most small businesses don't work but why most organizations, no matter how large or small, no matter what their industry, be they high tech, low tech, or no tech, be they outwardly successful or on a precipitous decline, are doomed to exist in a primarily dysfunctional condition.

I have also discovered that in trying to change their condition in the best ways they know how, most organizations are simply bound to recreate an equally dysfunctional system, despite their well-meaning commitment to do the very opposite.

How is this possible? How can so many highly skilled and motivated people produce so many disastrous results? It is my belief that most organizations lack the tools, the knowledge, and most important, the *understanding* they need in order to transform themselves. It is also my belief that the tools, knowledge, and especially the *understanding* they need are not available to them through the management rhetoric, programs, and processes that are forever being pitched and sold to them. And the reason they are not is because these "new" messages about management are built upon the same old expectations and the same old definition of what management is and isn't. And they're wrong.

What *is* needed, therefore, is a revolution in the idea of management: what it is, what it can be expected to do, and most certainly what it isn't. This book was written in the hope that I could share with you what my people and I have learned over the past two decades: how to provide the necessary insight into why most organizations don't work, and what to do about it. This information can be implemented by any organization, large or small.

Enter the idea of the E-Myth Manager.

The E-Myth Manager is an alternative to management as it is currently practiced.

The E-Myth Manager exercises full accountability and authority for the decisions he or she makes: he rigorously engages and teaches the people within his department or company (we'll call it an organization) to grow beyond their limitations; he expects all participants within his area of influence to participate fully in the development of the operating system of his organization, to contribute continuously to the innovation required to move the organization into a world-class state, to aid the organization in performing always at the "top of its class."

And the E-Myth Manager accomplishes all of these worthy objectives by operating his organization as if it were a business on its own, in the most entrepreneurial manner possible, outside the body politic of the larger firm, yet simultaneously serving the larger firm and *its* strategic initiatives by identifying the role his group must play to fulfill them, and playing out that role with conviction.

Therein lies the key to the E-Myth Manager's heart: conviction. Conviction that his life has meaning. Conviction that the people he is accountable for are fully engaged in whatever it is they are there to do. Conviction that the work they do together has meaning—not just that it is justifiable, but that it is important, and that everyone within the organization understands and agrees with that goal and is personally committed to it. Conviction that when a decision is made it is deemed a commitment, that once a commitment is made they will move mountains to keep it.

And the underpinning of that mind-set which the E-Myth Manager embodies, and that no Manager reading this book would argue with, is his commitment to thinking small. To thinking of his organization as a small business.

Therein we discover the success of the E-Myth

Manager. The E-Myth Manager is one who understands the profound difference between creating a *business* that works and getting a *person* to work—let alone *being* the person who works.

The E-Myth Manager is one who understands how critical it is to adopt an entrepreneurial mind-set, not only for the development of the business for which she is accountable, but for the lives of the people with whom she works.

The E-Myth Manager is also one who understands the profound difference one can make in any organization through the development and use of a management *system*, as opposed to the highly personal and subjective methods she is accustomed to using to get results.

Finally, the E-Myth Manager is one who forsakes forever the use of management rhetoric in order to produce a true transformation of everything she is committed to do. First, for the sake of herself. Second, for the sake of the organization of which she is determined to become an indelible part. And ultimately, for the sake of the people she comes into contact with on a day-to-day basis .

The order in which the E-Myth Manager's attention is placed bears repetition because that focus is critical to the challenge the E-Myth Manager faces in his attempt to transform the world around him.

For an E-Myth Manager, the focus is:

First, me.

Second, the organization of which I am a part.

Third, the people around me.

This focus is critical. For the law upon which it is based says that people are not selfless. Exactly the opposite is true. And if that is true, then how effective can any Manager be who has ignored his own human nature? The question each and every Manager must ask, and then answer, in order to begin the process the E-Myth Manager is committed to—that of true transformation—is not, What does my company want? Is not, What do my people want? But is, first and always foremost, What do *I* want? Truthfully. Honestly. Openly. Directly.

It is my hard-won belief that without asking that question—and then answering it—no one can be successful at managing anything. Because no one who has failed to ask, and then answer, that question will ever be able to manage himself.

The essence of the philosophy behind the E-Myth Manager is that if life is not being served in an organization by the Managers within it, then that organization isn't fit to work in.

The other component of being an E-Myth Manager is making choices. The choice of where I will work, and where I won't. The choice of what is of value, and what isn't. The choice of asking the questions, What does it mean to be an active human being? and, How do I engage in being that person?

These choices, this conviction, this commitment, and how to better understand not only the need for it, but the way in which to accomplish it, is what this book intends to describe.

With some effort, any organization that wishes to transform itself into a humanly productive entity, unlike most of the organizations around it, can and will create an entirely new operating reality—given the approach I am going to introduce to you here.

In short, this book provides a path not only to increased productivity, but to increased vitality, joy, and humanity in any organization that can find the heart and the resolve needed to rise above the ordinary, diminishing reality most organizations produce in everything and everyone they touch, no matter how lofty their mission statement might be.

Welcome to *The E-Myth Manager*.

INTRODUCTION

To venture causes anxiety, but not to venture is to lose one's self. . . . And to venture in the highest sense is precisely to become conscious of one's self.

Søren Kierkegaard

In my work with organizations large and small, I have observed and counseled, questioned and helped many Managers in need. Often their frustration stems from the apparent dysfunctionality of the environment or corporation in which they work, but perhaps more often the source of their angst and malaise is less obvious but even more insidious. Feeling trapped and underappreciated, they no longer derive any sense of meaning or purpose from what they do, nor do they feel any investment or ownership in the organization for which they work.

This cry can take as many forms as there are individual Managers—some get angry and lash out at their employees, their bosses, their families and friends; others internalize it and shut down emotionally, resulting in distant relationships both in and out of the workplace; still others work themselves to the point of physical and mental exhaustion with the hope that busying themselves by "doing more and doing better" will cure them of their ills.

What many of these Managers don't realize is that to effect true change within the organization, they must first change within—and that the ability to do that, and to subsequently reinvent the very jobs in which they find themselves, is primarily a matter of mind-set rather than of performance.

Few would dispute that management as we have come to know it rarely works, and on the chance that it does work, it rarely works well; thousands of professionals, ranging from management consultants to organizational psychologists, have made a healthy living writing, talking about, and debating this point.

I myself am one of them. Yet my perspective on management is really quite different, as I have spent much of my time working on and around *small* businesses, which, while having their own problems, are slightly different creatures from their cousins, mid-sized and large companies.

What I have discovered is that no matter what the size of the organization, it is the ability to treat the organization as a small business—and the Manager as a small-business owner—that produces a profound shift in the mind-set within that organization, from the very top to the very bottom. And with that shift in mind-set comes a very productive shift not only in results, but in the state of being of the people producing those results. That's what we'll attempt to do in this book.

As is fitting, at the opening of the book we'll venture back to the metaphorical birth of management, where we'll meet the first CEO (otherwise known as the Emperor) in the history of the world—and unearth the arbitrary origins of the management construct that we have come to regard as daily life. We'll see how management is highly subjective (rather than objective, as we have come to believe it is), restrictive (rather than liberating), and reactive (rather than entrepreneurial).

We'll also meet one Manager whose name is Jack—a fictional composite of many real-life Managers I have known throughout the years. As the director of field operations at The E-Myth Academy—my very own organization—Jack represents the best there is to offer in the stories and personalities of Managers who have come and gone from The

Academy, as well as those who have stayed and thrived.

A family man with a lovely wife named Annie and two small children, Jack is devoted to his job at The Academy, where he oversees seven employees. His job is to manage and develop the system of external certified consultants who are rapidly being deployed by The Academy throughout the world.

Reliable and committed, Jack had come to The Academy from a high-pressure, fast-track job where he never felt there was the time—or frankly, the inclination—to get the job done right.

And while he knew his previous job wasn't going to last a lifetime, during the five years he was there he gave as much as he had to give, often working well into the evenings, past his children's bedtimes, and through the weekend, like all Managers in the fast-track organizations around us are given to do.

Still, whatever he did wasn't enough to keep him or *his* Managers happy; and as a result, he felt used, depressed, and without purpose.

When I first talked to Jack seriously, he'd been working at The Academy for less than two years, and already he was feeling the wear and tear of it. The job he'd considered a godsend when he'd first accepted it had become routine, uninspiring, and somewhat of a constant frustration. Whereas at the beginning he'd been excited to go to work in the morning, he now found himself sleeping late, forgetting important meetings and assignments, and spending less time with his family but getting less done at work. Rather than being interested in how he could create greater productivity and success in the expanding network of consultants he was accountable for, he became more and more focused on how to make his job easier; which to him meant to work fewer hours and to make more money doing it.

As a result of that mind-set, Jack's people had become increasingly more difficult to motivate, the profitability of his division was down, and he had neither the tools nor the emotional impetus to fix it.

Embracing the irony of counseling one of my very own Managers, I became a source of solace for Jack, and he became my welcome companion, or alter ego, for the transformative journey that's become this book. You'll see a lot of direct interaction, in the form of dialogue, with Jack throughout the chapters—and whenever possible or appropriate, I will provide background and insight into him, as a person first and as a Manager second.

You'll see why, in his transformation from Manager into E-Myth Manager, it was necessary for Jack to explore his personal connections to the idea of management, from the time he was a little boy up through his time at The E-Myth Academy. And you'll see how and why everything Jack thought to be true of managing an organization is, in fact, false.

Throughout Part 1, Jack and I will explore what the discipline of management has become and why it no longer works. We'll also talk about the motivation of the Manager and the philosophy behind reinventing his role. In Part 2, we'll discuss, step by step, how a Manager such as Jack—or such as yourself—can become an E-Myth Manager, in an effort to find greater joy, meaning, and yes, productivity and profitability in your organization.

What I discovered in writing this book is that in my rush to invent an extraordinarily innovative organization, I overlooked the most critical part of the job: to understand the relationship of people to the process, and how to engage those people in my Vision without disenfranchising them in the process.

I trust you too will enjoy what Jack and I discovered together.

PART 1

THE DEATH AND
DYING OF
AMERICAN MANAGEMENT

THE MANAGERIAL MYTH

Intellectually, people may aspire for emancipation or enlightenment but emotionally they love small bondages around them. . . . They feel satisfied by knowing about liberation, reading about it, imagining it. They feel satisfied about this because the word liberation *has its own intoxication, the emotional feel about the meaning of the word has an intoxication.*

Vimala Thakar,
"Set Them on Fire!" A Portrait of a Modern Sage

At the beginning of every organization, of every business, of every invention—of every life—is an idea. An idea that is good, or an idea that is bad, an idea that is yet to be proven, but still, an idea.

Look at your own life. Who you are is no magical accident—if you look closely, you will see that your life represents ideas others have had that influenced you, for better or worse, ideas *you* have had that have influenced who you became, and even ideas you never even knew had influenced you. Like the idea of relativity. The idea of gravity. The idea of human equality. The idea of time. The idea of space. The idea of God. The idea of justice. The idea of management.

Certainly each and every one of these ideas has influenced your life to some degree, yet how many of these concepts have you questioned? Perhaps in the early years of your life you did. But as we know, the older we get, the less we have time for serious questions. As we get older, the most serious of questions become unserious answers; we've got a job to do, and we do it. Yet it is these very serious questions, these very ideas, that shape the work that men and women do. That shape each and every one of us as managers.

History teaches us that an unchallenged idea can be a dangerous proposition. Still, every day, tens of thousands, even hundreds of thousands, of managers just like you go to work in an organization founded upon someone's idea and assume the responsibility of making *something* happen. Whether or not the idea is still viable, still achievable, still sane.

It doesn't matter what kind of company or which kind of department or division you manage—the fact that you're trying to manage it at all is, based upon my experience, insane. Management, as we have come to know it, is the product of many years of insanity based on an idea that to manage means to strive to *control everything around us*. Something humans were never born to do.

It is my belief that our idea of management dates back as far as people do, thousands upon thousands of years, as do our ideas of power, of work, and of prestige; our ideas of systems and bosses and careers; our ideas of what it means to have a job and what it means to lose one.

And at the top of the list is the idea of what it means to be a Manager.

THE ACCIDENTAL BIRTH OF MANAGEMENT

The idea of the Manager is best typified by the illustration on the following page. It shows the pyramids being built. It shows the workers, their immediate Managers (today we call them supervisors), and the supervisors' Managers. The supervisors are the guys with the whips and chains. The workers, in case it isn't obvious, are the ones moving 400 billion tons of

monster rock into place to build the pyramid for their great leader.

As the story goes, the very entrepreneurial leader of this gambit was lying around one day eating grapes and cavorting with women and boys when it suddenly occurred to him that he wouldn't get to do this forever. That, at some point, he was going to die. "There must be some way to memorialize my magnificence," he thought, "to make me immortal." He wondered for a moment, then exclaimed, "What about a great big rock or temple, or—I've got it— what about a *pyramid!* An Emperor's tomb. The biggest box anyone has ever been put to rest in. Bigger than anything anyone has ever built before. Bigger than a mountain."

Ah, the grapes must have tasted sweeter as this idea—this bigger-than-any-idea-he-had-ever-had-before idea—took form in his mind. And from the moment the idea possessed him, he lived with that picture in his mind, he ate with it in mind, he slept with it in mind. No matter what, he had to do it!

So he gathered together his ministers (the senior management team), his overseers (the middle management team), and his foremen (the supervisors). And he placed the execution of his precious Vision in the hands of the guys who carried the whips and chains and knew how to use them.

So the Emperor sucked on grapes while the senior Managers worried about the numbers and the middle Managers walked around with clipboards and made not-so-idle threats. And the subordinates, by the millions, dug up rock, inhaled rock, ate rock, spit out rock, swallowed rock, picked up rock, and moved rock toward its final destination, where they hoisted rock, shifted rock, lifted rock, balanced rock, and placed rock upon rock upon rock upon rock. Meanwhile, miraculously, the grand pyramid rose, out of sand, out of an idea as thin as the air between the ears of the Emperor, manifested from virtually nothing into the most magnificent something anyone had ever seen.

And in fulfilling the dreams of one man, other men began to dream of other grand ideas. If he could do that, they reasoned, why couldn't we do this? And that? And some other thing?

Like build the Great Wall of China. Or stage the Russian Revolution. Or create McDonald's, or Microsoft, or CNN?

All of these, built in the same way as that very first pyramid.

THE PLIGHT OF THE MODERN MANAGER

Today's Emperors—we call them visionaries—rely upon a "new" model of management, which, while not really any different from the old model, does feature a couple of new twists: one is the technological revolution, which is forcing us all to do more faster; the other is the aftermath of reengineering, which is forcing us to do more with fewer people.

No wonder modern-day Managers are so depressed.

In the absence of "elbows and shoulders," the people who moved the rock and were lost to down-sizing, Managers became the Emperors' lackeys. They embraced the challenge in earnest. They bought business books and management treatises written by consultants and academics who trans-lated the realities of the real world. They attended management trainings and seminars and workshops, to hear themselves being applauded as the twentieth century's new profession. Like physicians and attor-neys and the clergy, Managers felt they were making a significant contribution to society and to the world at large, and business was fast becoming a new church. They called where they worked a "culture." They spoke of "quality" and "core values" and "mis-sions." They talked about uncovering the "soul" of the organization. They talked about "spirit" and "meaning," and sent their people to "vision quests." They learned about leadership and went to Utah to learn to distinguish themselves from ordinary Man-agers as extraordinary leaders. They learned there was a science to it all. That leaders are made not born. That you could learn the seven essential skills, or the six effective habits, or the trick of becoming a one-minute Manager. They listened in earnest and learned all the tricks, and still nothing changed, because the Managers—and the gurus who were teaching them—were only treating the symptoms, not the causes.

MEET JACK, A GUY JUST LIKE YOU

Jack was one such Manager. Raised by his mother, a teacher, and his father, a loyal organization man, Jack grew up with management. His father's boss came over once a week for dinner. His mother socialized with the wives of his father's coworkers. To him, business equaled a blue suit and white shirt, eight-hour days, and dinner on the table by five for his father, who'd worked at the same corporation his entire life.

There had always been a kind of allure about management for Jack, and his father recognized this early on. He had egged Jack on even as a small boy, taking him to the office on occasional Fridays, introducing him to his staff and encouraging him to "manage" rather than just "play" store when Jack and his friends got together after school. An inquisitive student, Jack scored straight As throughout intermediate and high school, and went to Stanford University, where he majored in business and management. At the same time, he took a job as an assistant store

Manager at the campus bookstore to help pay his way through school. He couldn't have been more thrilled.

He liked working as much as studying, that was certain. But the job wasn't what he'd thought it would be. The long hours and the mindless stacking were bad enough, but then there was Cody, the Manager of the bookstore, who had a way of making Jack feel bad. First, he'd told Jack he was lucky to have a job, that Cody was providing him with the best education he'd ever get. As time went by, Jack began to feel more like a slave to the whims and whimsy of Cody, rather than a valued employee. No matter how hard Jack worked, Cody raised the bar, and his evaluations of Jack's performance often had little to do with the work actually being done. In spite of this, Jack stuck it out. He needed the money to get through school, and the devil he knew, he thought, was surely better than the devil he did not. He had also learned "not to be a quitter" from his father, who'd said, "Your career is who you are. It's the path to financial, psychological, and cultural security."

Jack eventually graduated from school, got married, and got his first "real" job, as an assistant sales Manager of a major department store. He was glad to have left Cody and the bookstore behind, and happy to throw himself wholly into the first illustrious step of his career. This first step on the corporate ladder wasn't accomplished with great flourish, however; rather, it was a quiet, thoughtful, and unassuming one. The store was close to the small apartment he had rented with his new wife, Annie; the pay was good, and the challenge, great. Jack resolved to give everything he had—and then some—to succeed in his first real corporate role.

And succeed he did. He did what was asked of him. He pushed the limits of his personal life to accomplish tasks that were beyond the duty of an assistant sales Manager. He gave up his time, often studying into the night and working long hours every day. He even moved with his now growing family, three times during that first step, once across country, once to the Midwest, once back to where he'd started from. He became someone who could be depended upon to do the job well.

As reward, he was promoted three times, received more perks, benefits, salary, and bonuses, and gradually moved up the corporate ladder. Unbeknownst to Jack, however, his life was fast becoming a cliché. But he truly didn't notice—in part, because he was just too busy, but also because deep down inside him there resided an earnestness he couldn't account for, a need to be needed, to be relevant, to play a serious part in the life around him. Deep inside he thought he was doing exactly the right thing. He saw the signs, after all. The company grew. His people respected him. He felt a certain sense of growing dignity.

Jack even felt a sense of purpose in what he was doing. He identified with the company, his bosses, and their goals, which, he believed, were his goals too. And for a while, perhaps, they genuinely were. But to a large extent, Jack's so-called happiness was dependent on a few very significant things: the largesse—or lack thereof—of his superior, whose own Vision all but ruled Jack's working life; Jack's own *idea* of management, which was influenced by many factors, including his father and his first boss; and Jack's lack of real motivation to do anything beyond what others expected of him.

When I first met Jack, as a Manager at my own company, The E-Myth Academy, he'd just about had it with management, period. As luck would have it, I happened upon a visibly despondent Jack when I was "walking around" my business, as Tom Peters had exhorted me to do. Jack was pacing outside of another Manager's office as he waited for her to get off the phone. With his face red and shiny, I could tell he was about to explode.

"What's going on with you?" I asked him.

"Uh, oh . . . nothing I can't handle," he replied nervously.

"You look to me like a guy who's harboring a lot of pent-up frustration."

"Ah, no . . . it's just . . ." He looked away.

"It's okay," I replied. "I see guys like you all the time, although usually in other people's companies. But in *my* company it's a lot harder to see, so I probably avoid it like the plague. What do you say we grab some lunch and get some of this negative energy out into the open so we can both take a look at it in earnest?"

Jack looked both terrified and relieved.

"Okay," he replied. "Let me get my coat."

2

THE MOTIVATION

OF THE MANAGER

. . . the passions that enslave us, the hidden motives that can pervert us, and the illusions that can blind us.

**Douglas Labier, Modern Madness: The Hidden Link
Between Work and Emotional Conflict**

I took Jack to a favorite coffee shop not far from The Academy offices in Santa Rosa, where we ordered coffee and sandwiches. Looking around nervously, he shifted uneasily in his seat. He was obviously not at all comfortable with the idea of discussing whatever was bothering him with me, the Emperor of the organization for which he worked. And I was intrigued, given how much experience I'd had helping other organizations and Managers solve their problems, to find a perfect specimen in my own backyard.

I decided to relieve him of the silence that stood between us.

"So, Jack," I started. "We don't know each other very well, but I'd like to help with whatever's bothering you, if I can. So why don't you start off by telling me what that might be."

"It's nothing, really," he replied. "I mean, nothing that I haven't dealt with many times before."

"Is it a particular project? A coworker? A client?"

"No, no, nothing like that. It's me . . . really, I'll be fine."

I had suspected all along that the look of utter exasperation—which comes only from an intense, accumulated emotional reaction—was the result of something having to do with Jack, not a client or coworker. In fact, my guess was that he had just about had it with his job as director of field operations. So I asked him.

"Is it your job that's bothering you?"

He brightened with recognition for a moment; then a cloud came over his face. He clearly wasn't sure what to say.

"It's okay, Jack. Forget for the time being who you think I am. For the moment, just pretend to yourself that I'm here as a consultant and friend. Tell me what's been going on."

He lifted his glass, took a swallow of water, and began.

THE EMPEROR MEETS THE EMPEROR

"The trouble is, I'm not exactly sure what's wrong," Jack started. "But I can tell you how I feel. My whole life, I've been raised to be a Manager. Some people have doctors in their families, some have lawyers. Between my father, his brothers, and their father, I have Managers. It may sound crazy to say, but it's really all I've ever wanted to do."

"That's not crazy," I offered.

Jack continued, "And for the first decade of my professional career, I was a Manager—and a damn good one. I loved being involved with the people above, the people beneath. I worked really hard—sometimes, maybe too hard—but I was rewarded and I felt like I was doing something meaningful."

Jack stopped. It was clear he was afraid to continue, but I urged him on.

"Okay. So I left my first real job—which I loved—

when I got a better offer. That didn't work out. And just when I didn't know where to turn, I got the job at The Academy. It was a godsend—convenient, interesting, and, I thought, maybe actually functional! And it really is a great place to work."

"But you're just not happy?" I asked.

"I was," Jack added. "I'm just not anymore. Productivity in my department is down. Profits are low. I don't connect with my people, and I don't feel any great joy in what I do. It's like I have to shut myself off when I get here so that I can assume the persona of someone else."

"It's not a persona you're assuming," I told him, getting a very clear picture of the problem. "It's a Vision."

"A Vision?" He looked genuinely perplexed.

"Yes," I said. "You come here and you assume your role in implementing my Vision. The Vision of the Emperor."

"But I believe in this company, I do!" Jack argued. "I just don't feel invested. The work gets harder, the opportunities seem to be getting more limited, and my people seem to be more closed off when, in fact, the E-Myth Consultant network is growing at record speed. What's worse is that, at the same time that I'm their Manager and should know how to get them to be different, I'm feeling more and more just like them. What do I do?"

"It's time to become your own Emperor, Jack. And I'm going to teach you how to do it. Because if you *don't* do it, Jack, if you don't learn how to become your own Emperor, if you continue as you always have, serving the Visions of others rather than your own, your life won't be worth a plugged nickel."

THE MANAGER BECOMES AN EMPEROR

How—and why—does a Manager become his own Emperor? That's the subject of this book. Because any Manager who can learn to think like an Emperor is indeed thinking like an Entrepreneur. And the E-Myth Manager is an entrepreneurial Manager who acts as if he "owns" his organization, separate and distinct from the organization at large.

How do you go about doing this? First, the nature of your work must change. And for your work to change, your attachment to the force that is driving everything you do must change. You must come to the realization—the very personal under-standing—that despite what you have been led to believe, there is no real mission statement or business aim that's propelling you to do the things you are supposed to do. It's not the company and its goals that are motivating you, it's some *person*. It's not Microsoft you're here to serve, it's Bill Gates. No matter what the company tells you. It's not Apple you're here to serve, it's Steve Jobs. No matter what the company tells you. It's not The E-Myth Academy you're here to serve, it's Michael Gerber. No matter what the company tells you. To fail to understand this truth presupposes objectivity where only the subjective is true. When a Manager understands that satisfying a *person's*—his boss's—aim is what his job is truly all about, the whole job changes. Suddenly, and probably for the very first time, the truth comes into focus. And when the truth comes into focus for a Manager, he is first given the exciting opportunity to ask the only question that can save him:

Am I here to serve this person, or am I here to serve me?

THE EMPEROR'S SEDUCTION

But as we all know, the Emperor is a very seductive person. Bill Gates knows exactly what he wants. And because he is very clear in knowing and articulating what he wants, he focuses his aim on those who can get it for him. Usually, the Manager.

Not so with the Manager. The Manager may have her own big ideas for herself, for the organization, but when it comes right down to it, no matter how clear or passionate or intent she is on realizing these goals, the Manager is not the Emperor.

Unlike the Emperor, the Manager is looking for a purpose, which provides her the opportunity she either does not know how, or is too afraid, to create for herself. The Emperor's purpose is big, his enthusiasm, catchy, the force behind it, full of steam, power, Vision, and passion. The Emperor's Vision is expansive.

And like a fly in a spider's web, the Manager is soon caught in the power of the Emperor's Vision.

When that happens, the Manager—with her own goals, dreams, and Vision—is lost, as she dedicates herself to bringing the Emperor's exciting new Vision to fruition.

Such is the seduction of the Emperor. It takes away the Manager's hope and replaces it with the Emperor's intention.

Every Manager has experienced this, but few think about the trade-off or understand at the moment of acquiescence the price they are about to pay for giving themselves up.

THE E-MYTH MANAGER

THE FIRST STEP IS ADMITTING THE PROBLEM

Of course, no one is doing this intentionally. The Emperor simply plays out his part, and the Manager simply plays out her part—both parts having been written eons ago. In most instances there is no evil or ill-will intended. As Ogden Nash would have said, it's not a sin of commission, but a sin of omission.

Which is exactly why it is so important to understand this long-standing relationship if you have any interest at all in changing your life. Understanding this law is where the Manager's opportunity to reinvent her life and the role she plays in her organization begins anew.

* * *

Jack and I got down to business quickly. He had loosened considerably once he realized I was sincere in my willingness to help, and he was intrigued by the idea of the Emperor.

"The Emperor is the owner of the Vision you've been instructed to manifest," I told him. "In this case, that Vision is mine. The first thing I want you to do is forget about me for a moment. Let's think about you."

"Okay," said Jack. "What now?"

"I want you to try to imagine what it means to be an Emperor. Not to be me—but that you are your *own* Emperor. Think about what it might mean to really have a purpose of your own, and only your own—not something you're happy to toss aside for the safety of realizing someone else's purpose, but a purpose as huge as the pyramid that that very first Emperor so long ago envisioned in the absence of such an unthinkable thing. To begin reinventing your work as a Manager, you must begin the job of reinventing yourself."

*   *   *

This is where the Manager's mind must focus its attention.

Which is what the mind's *intention* must be: to understand the power of *attention*.

Which is how one begins to escape from the safe, seductive clutches of the organization, of the Emperor's Vision, which is first, foremost, and always about his need to get more of everything than anyone ever needed. It is he who has the imagination and the presence of mind to seduce others into the Domain of Getting.

It is the Domain of Getting that has inspired the creation of all of the management tools we use today.

GOING BEYOND THE DOMAIN OF GETTING

Getting is the motivation behind nearly everything we do.

And so, to go beyond getting, one must first understand the role of getting, and the tools we use to enable us to become skilled at it.

Every enterprise on the face of the earth has as its sole purpose to become a world-class player in the Domain of Getting. And it is every Emperor's wish to be a dominant player in the Domain of Getting. When Donald Trump boasts about his accomplishments, all he's really doing is establishing his early ascent to the role of Trump the Emperor, a heavy hitter in the Domain of Getting. Being taken very seriously—*by other heavy hitters*—is an important part of the game. Bill Gates could not imagine not being taken seriously as the most influential man of this age. Steve Jobs is determined to be taken seriously for his turnaround of Apple, even though he continues to tell the entire world that that's not what he's there to do. If he told them he was there to do that, and failed, his serious-player status would take a nosedive. And heavy hitters like Steve Jobs can't tolerate that kind of nosedive. The Domain of Getting is all about ego. Huge egos create huge pyramids. Small egos create small pyramids. Insignificant egos get lost in the game.

"But what does the Domain of Getting have to do with my becoming my own Emperor?" Jack asked. "I mean, it's not like I have any chance of becoming Donald Trump."

"You certainly have a chance at that, Jack," I answered. "The question is, is that what you want? And your answer to that question will tell you everything you need to know about yourself and the Domain of Getting."

THE TOOLS OF YESTERDAY AND TODAY

The Domain of Getting has inspired Managers to create a host of tools, which are very much the same today as they were generations ago. The tools, of course, were created to further the Emperor's stature in the Domain of Getting.

Yet, despite Managers' good intentions, and how seriously the media have taken these tools, it is critical for the Manager who wishes to escape the insane world he has unwittingly found himself in to note that *none of these tools work!*

Not motivation. Not empowerment. Not quality.

Not teams. Not learning to listen. Not leadership training. Not open book management. Not seven habits. Not walking on fire. Not reengineering. Not anything you've read about in a business magazine, despite everyone's avowed commitment to it when it happens to be the rage. No, I'm here to tell you that none of these work, because they are missing the point by a mile. These tools represent a pseudo-science of management that exists only in the imaginations of countless Managers who have been seduced to look at everything but the truth. And the truth is this:

The only management tools that have *ever* worked were invented at the beginning of time. They are greed and fear.

"Greed and fear are what inspire the Emperor to construct a larger-than-life pyramid," I told Jack. "Greed and fear are what compel the modern equivalent of 'elbows and shoulders'—Managers—to show up at work every day, or not. Greed and fear are what prevent you from becoming your own Emperor. Throughout the history of the world, greed and fear have *always* worked as motivators. There's a mantra of stupidity that Swami Chetanananda has attributed to all of mankind—the common, plaintive, heartrending refrain, *'What's going to happen to me?'* That is what has always kept us awake at night.

"That is why the first step toward reinventing your work as a Manager is to understand and accept the truth that greed and fear are running rampant in every organization you have ever been in—including ours, Jack—and every organization you will ever be in. Until *you* change it. Until you take full responsibility for your own life, until you take full responsibility for freeing yourself psychologically from not only me, your present Emperor, but from every Emperor like me, your life will never change. Until you become your own Emperor, until you find the courage to take charge of your own Vision, until you look fear and greed squarely in the face and understand how they have brought you to where you are; until you do that, nothing, but absolutely nothing, will make any difference. The questions you need to ask are just two: Where's the fear? Where's the greed?"

"That's easy," said Jack. "The fear is a constant in me, and has been since I was a child. I picked up on my mother's fear of financial insecurity pretty early on—which only fueled my father's fear of unemployment. 'Your career is all you have,' he'd tell me. 'Don't screw it up.' That philosophy has haunted me my whole life.

"But I'd never thought I was greedy until I was hired away from my first real job. That feeling of being wanted, by someone who wanted to pay me *twice* what I was making! Of course I deserved it, I reasoned. And though it was painful, I left a job I loved for a fast-track position with rising-star potential. Boy, was I sorry.

"The five years I stayed there were the worst of my life. Sure, the money was good, but the work! It never, ever stopped. Fifteen-hour days were the norm; people were in, people were out. And no one had any clear sense of what we were supposed to be doing!"

"Fear and greed are normal reactions, Jack," I reassured him. "But the question you must ask yourself is, How have fear and greed held me back in my life? Take some time to think about it—the very fear we are talking about often serves as a fortress to protect what deep down inside we really want. And that, my friend, is the first step to becoming an E-Myth Manager."

3

Reinventing the Work

of the Manager

New ways of thinking about familiar things can release new energies and make all manner of things possible.

Charles Handy, The Age of Unreason

Recognizing the myth of management—and the motivation of most Managers—is a healthy step toward applying the entrepreneurial mind-set to your job—that is, becoming an E-Myth Manager. But taking action and beginning to reinvent the work that you do is often the hardest step to take. The following rules will guide you in your quest to give up the drug of Emperor dependence. These are the rules that shape your life as an E-Myth Manager, and consequently, influence your relationship with everyone around you. I call them the Seven Rules of Management Independence. They are:

1. Know what you want.
2. Know you have the power get it.
3. There can be no causes other than your own.
4. If you cannot manage yourself you cannot manage anything.
5. There are no simple answers, only complex questions.
6. Before it gets better it is going to get worse.
7. These rules must become the defining principles of your life.

THE SEVEN RULES OF MANAGEMENT INDEPENDENCE

RULE 1: KNOW WHAT YOU WANT.

Jack and I had finished our lunch and were driving back to the office when he asked about the differences between the Emperor's Vision and its execution by the organization.

"The true Emperor," I said (quickly establishing the fact that there are true Emperors and bogus Emperors), "is obsessed with his Vision. He knows what he wants. And he will not give up till he gets it. The Manager's interpretation of the Emperor's Vision, on the other hand, is only a pale reflection of the Emperor's want. And because the Manager's idea of what the Emperor wants is only a reflection of the original Vision, it can't possibly pack the punch or the force of the Emperor's Vision. As the Emperor's Vision travels down through the organization, it becomes increasingly reflective and decreasingly intense. But a Vision is not something a Manager is expected to think about; it is something to be executed. Something the Manager is supposed to implement. No sooner is there a Vision than there is work to do. And every Manager knows what that means. It means that no matter how unsure he is about what he is supposed to do, his job is to do it anyway. His Manager is waiting. And her Manager is waiting. And the Emperor is waiting. Everybody is waiting on everyone else to fulfill the Emperor's Vision.

"The Manager does the only thing he can do. He matches the Emperor's obsession with his own compulsion by working twice as hard as is reasonable. By pushing his people twice as hard as he should. By living every hour as if it were his last. By breaking schedules and remaking schedules. By doing everything to excess to match the excess of the Emperor's expectation. It isn't long before everyone in the organization is hopelessly caught up in the vision's sway, in the Emperor's mania, in the passion of the moment. Nothing is more important. Nothing is more vital to the success of everyone in the organization. The Emperor's Vision becomes the purpose of everyone's lives."

Jack barely let me finish my thought before he jumped in. "That's fine," he said. "But what if I don't know what I want?"

"If a Manager's *want* can only be understood as a reflection of the Emperor's want, and that only as translated through a hierarchy of Managers between them, then it can be truthfully said that the Manager has no life of his own at all! His life becomes a mere reflection—and in most cases, a very pale reflection—of the expectations others have of him.

"You may be put off by the idea of having to know what you want," I continued. "And it may take a while to figure it out. But until you do, you will be no closer to owning your job, to managing your organization, or to increasing your enjoyment of what you do. To fulfill your potential, to be more than a mere reflection of someone else's Vision, it is absolutely essential for you—and each and every Manager like you—to learn how to *match* the Emperor's intensity, rather than reflect it. And the only way a Manager can honestly do that is through the pursuit of his *own* Vision."

*　　*　　*

I asked Jack to think back over his life and point to something that he really wanted.

"Aside from wanting to be a Manager, I'd always dreamed about going to Stanford," he said.

"And you did it," I offered. "You had a Vision, a picture of yourself graduating from Stanford. You chose to make the next stage of your life's work to turn that Vision into a reality; you determined what it would take to be successful in your quest; you followed the course of action indicated; you overcame the host of transient emotions that are bound to accompany one moving toward their Vision, like frustration, depression, exhaustion, anger, doubt, confusion, and so forth; you graduated from Stanford.

"The point is that you would have implemented identically the same process if it had been the Emperor's Vision you were pursuing. The only difference is that when you've completed *your* process, as opposed to the Emperor's, *you* own it. Every bit of intelligence garnered in the process, every skill enhanced in the process, is to your benefit. It's *your* intelligence. *Your* skill. *Your* transformation. Through which to create a *new* Vision for yourself."

Jack paused. I took the opportunity to complete my thought.

"Do you see, Jack, that by becoming your *own* Emperor, by creating your *own* Vision, by knowing clearly what it is *you* want—before *ever* considering what the *Emperor* wants—you have freed yourself from your compulsion, you have freed yourself from his obsession, you have taken the first step to becoming a successful, fulfilled, independent person?

"In other words, Jack," I said as forcefully as I dared in the moment, "*the responsibility of every Manager is to become the significant force behind his own life by choosing to be his own Emperor.*"

I stopped the car, and asked Jack a difficult question.

"So, you got Stanford, and you got the position you wanted with a major department store, and you got the life you wanted by getting married and moving back to Sonoma County and getting a job at The E-Myth Academy.

"But having said all that, Jack, do you see that those Visions are simply intermediate benchmarks in something *called* 'Jack's life,' but that they are *not* Jack's life? And if the benchmarks we've just identified are *not* Jack's life, do you see that there is something much bigger in question here *called* Jack's life?"

"I think so," Jack said.

"Well, then," I continued, "it is critical for you to understand it; otherwise it will do you no good. The thing you need to understand is that *the Emperor's Vision is always bigger than the benchmarks; that's where the intensity comes from.*

"Without the intensity, there can be no realization of the Vision. And for there to be life-size intensity in your Vision, Jack, your Vision has got to be much more than simple objectives, much more than simple intermediate benchmarks. Your Vision has got to take in the entirety of your life, the entire product of your life, as well as the process of it. And to do *that* you must be able to enVision your life as a whole. As one complete thing. As a galaxy within which the forces of your life play out their roles. As a creation. Your own creation. An invention only you can conceive.

"That's what separates the Emperor from his Managers. The Emperor's Vision takes in an entire enterprise, while the Manager's Vision includes only fragments of one. To become your own Emperor you must learn to see your life through a wide-angle lens.

And to do that, you must learn to take your own life, your own Vision, as seriously as you would take mine.

"So, having said all *that*, Jack," I said, unbuckling my seat belt, "the question is, *Now* what do you do?"

RULE 2: KNOW YOU HAVE THE POWER TO GET IT.

Jack answered, "I'm not sure."

I said, "But do you see that unless you are sure, you will never find the means to get it?"

"I think so . . . yes," he said.

"And do you also see," I continued, "that unless you are absolutely clear about what you want, and that what you want must be wanted with everything you have so that it's big enough to require all of your intention, you will always be an open target for someone *else's* intention, someone *else's* Vision, someone *else's* game? And that that's what happens to all of us? People need a game to play in life; people hunger for purpose. Without their own, they are immediately distracted into the misguided belief that anyone's purpose will do. But it *won't* do. Not by a long shot.

"You've seen that yourself, Jack. This 'thing' you can't describe—feeling out of control, unsuccessful, unfulfilled. You have fallen into the Manager's trap—

at The E-Myth Academy, of all places. It's easy to do, but the consequences are no less deadly. The Manager's trap is the passive relinquishment of your personal responsibility for creating your own purpose, your own Vision, your own life. In your case, you found a purpose at The E-Myth Academy that you willingly accepted as your own. You then went on like a good soldier, committed to The Academy's purpose, my purpose, just as if it was your own. You took beachheads, you took enemy encampments, you fought fights you never created, and won each and every time—all for The Academy, all for the Vision, all for me. And I thank you for it. The only problem is that after you have done this for a number of more years, one day, if you are lucky, you will wake up at your desk, or during a conversation, or while driving to work, just like Rip Van Winkle, and you will say to yourself, 'Who am I? Where am I? What happened?'"

"You're right," Jack admitted, somewhat sadly.

"And suddenly the absence of a personal purpose, a personal Vision, a *life of your own*, will become the void in which you find yourself. But even though you've awakened, unless you're very, very lucky, it will be too late to do anything about it. Because you will have spent your best years and your best energy pursuing my Vision, The Academy's Vision, dressed up like your very own. The energy, the intensity you'll need to get back on track, on the track of your own life, will have been lost in false pursuit.

"You will have become so entrenched in my Vision that you will have lost your ability to distinguish yourself from it. You will have come to believe that *my* purpose is *your* purpose, that *your* purpose is *my* purpose. And Jack, they *aren't*. Even though every Emperor for all time would want you to believe they are.

"Not only must you be certain of what you want— for yourself—you must also be certain that you understand the importance of this statement:

"Once you know what you want, only you can get it. You can't delegate the responsibility for inventing your own life."

RULE 3: THERE CAN BE NO CAUSES
OTHER THAN YOUR OWN.

Jack looked at me, obviously seeing in a flash the dilemma I was creating for him.

"So, what do I do with my passion for *your* cause, for *your* Vision?" he asked, almost sadly.

"My cause must become secondary to your cause," I said, realizing I had never said that to any employee before, and feeling at the same time what Jack must've been feeling as I was changing the rules of our game. A game he had loved and devoted himself to.

"If my cause is to truly be successful, it is absolutely essential for you to have a cause of your own that is significantly more important to you than mine is. Just as the Emperor has no causes to satisfy other than *his* own, you can have no other causes to satisfy other than *your* own. If you are to understand where the Emperor's intensity comes from, that is. The Emperor's intensity comes from his insatiable desire to have what he wants. To the degree your desire is a reflection of someone else's, rather than your own, your intensity will be a reflection as well. To experience the full weight of one's potential intensity, one must have one's own intensity, which in itself is only a product of what you want. But the two, the intensity and the want, go hand in hand. Without the want, the intensity burns itself out in useless activity, chasing minor wants. Chasing objectives. Without the intensity, the want finds itself languishing, going nowhere, experiencing greater and greater detachment from the person who conceived of it in the beginning, until, like an old electric bulb, the want simply dies out.

"Also, since the quality and quantity of energy is what constitutes your ability to persevere, it should be easier for you to understand why it is that when you attempt to split your attention between two wants, someone else's and your own, the force of energy available for either diminishes. Which is to say that:

"Without choosing to pursue your own cause, as opposed to someone else's, you make it impossible to live to your fullest potential, to fulfill your life's aim."

"You still haven't answered my question," Jack said. "What do I do about your Vision, and my passion for it? Are you suggesting that I've got to give up my passion for your cause altogether?"

"No. Because as long as you're working at The Academy, you'll still have to keep my Vision in mind. But you do have to engage yourself in a new direction in order to answer that question for yourself. I can't answer it for you. You've got to ask yourself, Does Michael Gerber's Vision enable me to fulfill my own goals? To pursue my own Vision at the same time as I pursue his? What's more, does Michael Gerber's Vision add value to my pursuit, or does it simply fail to interfere with it?

"In other words," I continued, "If my Vision doesn't serve you by adding energy and intensity to your own personal pursuits, then, candidly, there *should* be no future for us. That's why most Managers are dying on the job," I continued. "Because they have forsaken their own lives in order to fulfill someone else's Vision. All the time mistaking the word *career* for the word *life*.

RULE 4: IF YOU CANNOT MANAGE YOURSELF, YOU CANNOT MANAGE ANYTHING.

"There's a subset in all of this," I continued, "which is essential if any of the rules are to mean anything. And that is, in order to implement Vision, in order to manifest it in the day-to-day reality of your life, you must develop the capability of a Manager. To truly do that, you must first learn how to manage yourself. That's why you're feeling so out of sorts, Jack, you must first establish a relationship with yourself before you can tackle everything else a Manager is expected to do."

"I have to create a relationship with myself? I'm not sure what that means," Jack said as we approached the doorway to my office.

"Have a seat and I'll explain.

"There are three roles each and every Manager must play out every day if there is to be any balance in his life: the role of the Emperor, the role of the Manager, and the role of the Technician.

"Of course, all of us are familiar with the second and third roles, the Manager and the Technician, we play those all the time. At least we think we do. But we don't do them intentionally. We don't play them out with a full mind, aware of what role each plays in our grand scheme. We simply accept the work we do as a sort of coagulate of stuff. We do stuff, but we don't think of the stuff we do as distinctly belonging to the three roles. We don't say to ourselves, 'This is Management work, this is Technician work, this is the work of the Emperor.'

"And because we fail to differentiate one task from another, we also fail to *discriminate* between one task and another, which means we don't choose the work we do with a mind for the relative importance or unimportance of it, for the value it contributes to our Vision, or for the price it exacts. Which means we haven't created standards through which to monitor ourselves on a day-to-day basis.

"In order to manage yourself as a Manager and as a Technician, you must think in terms of standards as far as the work serves your Vision, or your aim.

"In the case of the Technician, there are two higher aims: the Technician's own personal aim, his own Vision; and the aim of his Manager, the Manager's Vision as it relates to the company in which they both work.

"In the case of the Manager, there are also two higher aims; his own personal aim, his own Vision; as well as the aim of his Manager and the company in which he works.

"The personal Vision of the Manager, and the personal Vision of the Technician in this case are both the same. After all, each is simply another part of the same human being. And that's where the Emperor comes in.

"The Emperor is the third force in this three-way relationship. The Emperor provides Vision and intensity while the Manager fulfills his accountability and the Technician fulfills his. We'll talk more about the work each of these roles is accountable for a little later on.

"Our work is to be conscious of the roles the Emperor, the Manager, and the Technician are playing—*as they are playing them*—as they go about their daily routines either fulfilling or disrupting this complex organization of wills, purposes, work, and relationships in this *system* we call our lives.

"So to manage oneself, Jack, it is necessary to think in terms of standards, and before you can think of standards, you must first have a Vision for yourself. This Vision should encompass who you wish to become—not who you *are*. But understand, if the person you see in your Vision is the same as the person you are, only doing something different, it is not a Vision, it is a dream. Bill Gates doesn't *dream* about Microsoft, he en*visions* it. He en*visions* a Microsoft universe. Understand, I'm not talking about the *content* of Bill Gates's Vision here, I'm talking about the *scale* of it. It's the *scale* of one's Vision that shapes one's life. When Fred Smith envisioned Federal Express, it was bigger than a bread box for sure. The Vision called FedEx was the motherlode of all visions. As was CNN. As was McDonald's. As was Einstein's Vision of relativity. As was Lao Tzu's Vision of the Tao.

"And so I bring to you the idea that there are no small people, only small visions. We're too easy on ourselves; too gentle. Not about everything, of course. We can be very hard on ourselves about all the little things in our lives. All the little things we should do, we should have, we should be.

"But I've seen from experience that all of that tension around the little things in our lives is a sure sign of our lack of a bigger Vision."

"I don't think I'm easy on myself at all," Jack replied.

"But you are, Jack," I said with special emphasis. "When I say we're too easy on ourselves, I mean that we are too willing to give ourselves up to the ordinary. The compulsions and obsessions that make up our lives. Our weight, our relationships, our IQ, our nose, our complexion. Or even worse, we give ourselves up to someone else's Vision. Or even worse than that, to no Vision at all, thinking that keeping busy is what life is all about.

"So, to manage anything, you must first learn to manage yourself. And to do so, we begin with a

Vision, create the standards against which we monitor our own behavior, know that our behavior is that of the Emperor, the Manager, and the Technician, and then begin to act in all three roles as though we are the person we're intending to be. And watch ourselves as we go through the process, day by day, hour by hour, minute by minute. Watch ourselves as we fail at it, as we succeed at it, as we forget what we're doing and why we're doing it. Watch ourselves with only one objective in mind: to see ourselves exactly as we are, and exactly as we wish ourselves to be, and to experience the gap between the two and the tension created by it.

"To watch ourselves with the eye of an objective observer—that is the purpose of Rule 4. By watching we will quickly discover that to think we are able to manage anything at all is sheer insanity. We can engage with it, we can connect with it, we can be interested in it, we can even learn some extremely valuable things about it, but we cannot control it, no matter how hard we try, or for how long.

RULE 5: THERE ARE NO SIMPLE ANSWERS, ONLY COMPLEX QUESTIONS.

"Rule 5 introduces the paradox into the equation, putting the entire *idea* of rules up for serious question. Rule 5 tells us that finding answers is not the purpose of the rules—or this journey—at all; *discovering what questions to ask is!*"

"How do you mean?" Jack asked.

"A few minutes ago, I asked you the question 'Now what?' And your answer was 'I'm not sure.' Of course, that's the only honest answer you could have given me. On the other hand, you could have told me that the answer was to create your own Vision. And of course, given what I've said up till now, that would have been an appropriate answer. Appropriate, but disingenuous. Because to say it is not to do it, or even to begin to understand the process. How? I would have then asked. How would you create your Vision?"

"I still don't know," Jack said.

"Right. So while I am saying it is essential for you to en*vision* your life in order to live it as fully as possible, I am also saying that most likely you have no idea about how to begin the process. Yet begin it you must. For if you don't, you are leaving your life up to chance, to the moods you feel, and the coincidences that prevail upon you, and the circumstances and conditions that move through the day and the night around you, to randomness and chaos, to forces that take you this way and that way your entire life. Just as we all have a tendency to do. You know what I mean, Jack. Everything in your life hasn't been about reaching benchmarks. In fact, I'm sure if we were to examine your life in detail, we would discover that most of it has been about finding out after the fact that what you *thought* you were going to do was markedly different from that which you *actually* did."

"I remember the plans that worked out," Jack said. "But the rest doesn't really stick with you."

I had no idea how long we had been sitting in my office, but I know the afternoon had quickly passed. I had calls to return, and Jack surely had much work to do—but something kept him glued to the chair in my office. I sensed a breakthrough.

Jack spoke.

"This is all pretty amazing," he said. "When I arrived here, at The Academy, I saw it as a rare gift. Like a surprise package that was handed to me when I most needed it, at a time in my life when I least expected it, because I didn't think I deserved it. My last job was so awful! And it has continued to mean that much to me. But now, I'm starting to wonder about what could have happened had I taken full responsibility for myself and my life before. *I know that I haven't*. I've always given myself up to my work, The Academy, and finally, in some fragmented way, you, even though we haven't spoken a hundred words to each other over the entire time I've been working for your company. Isn't that strange?" he said. "That I could know you as little as I do, and yet believe that I know you so intimately? So much so that I have entrusted my life to you?"

"Yes, isn't it," I answered him. "But it happens more often than we think. People give themselves up to the answers that present themselves in the form of solutions to their everyday problems. The answers come in the form of stories and dreams and illusions. They come out of the mouths of other people more certain of themselves than we are. Or, if not more certain, at least more able to act with certainty. You were sucked into The Academy—not totally because our intention was so overpowering, but also because yours was almost nonexistent. You wandered in and were caught, simply because the attraction of our positive energy was more attractive to you than the negative alternatives. Imagine, a management position right here in Sonoma County where you had just been married, wished to spend the rest of your life, and where there were no other such positions available. Was this a miracle? Could life really be so perfect? Could you actually have your cake and eat it too?"

Jack smiled broadly. He was seeing it just as I had described it. And yes, that's exactly how it had happened. 'What a stroke of luck!' he had thought.

"But at that moment, at the exact moment when you found an answer to an unasked question, the dream job with a dream company, in exactly the right place, offering you exactly the right opportunity, it was then that the answer, the opportunity, could have been put into serious question. The question, Yes, but what do I really want? Think about it Jack," I said. "You've been here two years. Two years out of your life. Two years completely absorbed in doing it, doing it, doing it. Doing this thing you do here at The Academy, but to what end? For what purpose? To serve you in what way? And what about the next year, and the next? Who are you, Jack, other than a consumer of goods, an intelligent, fair person, a person who gives the very best you've got, not only to The Academy, but to your consultants and your people? But what about you? Where are *you* in all this? What do *you* want? Don't you see that this question is liable to throw everything you take for granted, and have taken for granted up until now, on its head?

"So *now* what?" I asked, not expecting an answer.

"Rule 5 forces us to ask 'So now what?' just as we are getting comfortable. Just as we think we have the answers. Just as life begins to become predictable. Rule 5 forces us to remember that life is a continuous question, that in asking 'So now what?' we're reminded of where the energy is. It's in the questions, not in the answers. At least not until we are unable to ask questions, and the only answer is the end."

RULE 6: BEFORE IT GETS BETTER IT IS GOING TO GET WORSE.

As much as I hated to admit it, this rule truly hit the mark with my own personal experience. "Unfortunately, Jack, this is generally true in any transformative process worth its salt. Questioning shatters our belief in our own certainty, jostling our reality as if we were rag dolls. It is always a surprise when this happens, even if you feel you've prepared for it, even when you've asked for it, because you're suddenly a different person, and that's scary. You are questioning not just who your boss is and what his agenda is, but also everything you believed to be true, everything you were taught to be true, by your parents, by your teachers, by your bosses, whoever they were, and wherever you were working for them. Suddenly, nothing is familiar—the work you do, the career you've created, the money you've grown to need, the relationships you've forged, the words you use to describe your life's story, the understanding you have reached concerning parents, siblings, husband, wife, boss, Manager, subordinates, the job—all of this. Suddenly, and for no reason, you've questioned all of it. Because somehow you have to, even though it's terrifying.

"And in so doing, Jack, you just give up. That's all you can do. You give up the presuppositions and the preconceptions you've always 'known,' and you wipe the slate clean. For our mental salvation, we must ask, How do I spend my days, for what purpose, to what end; and where, in the middle of all that do I see myself as I truly am? When you do *that*, what can you expect but an enormous amount of pain?

"When we doubt, we try to get rid of the doubt as quickly as we can. When we want something, we gratify ourselves with it as quickly as we can. When we're afraid, we submerge it as quickly as we can. When we feel needed, we turn the situation into an opportunity to get something for ourselves as quickly as we can. How could the process of becoming honest, of becoming impartial, of becoming passionate, of uncovering who we really are and what we want be anything *but* painful? So it's going to feel worse before it feels better simply because of *the sheer, unadulterated shock of it!*"

"Why would I subject myself to such a process if I didn't really have to . . . it sounds horrible," Jack muttered.

"That's just it, Jack. You *do* have to. For the sake of your life, your sanity, and your livelihood. The shock should be something you enthusiastically pursue with the fever of a wild animal, as this kind of shock puts everything in your life and your work into perspective. This kind of shock causes you to remember yourself, and to commit yourself. And the message of this shock is that the only Emperor worth following is the one inside of you, the one who will not let you rest until you know who you are and why you do what you do. And then, when you're dissatisfied with the answer—as you will be, I assure you—then the Emperor inside will ask, So, *now*, Jacko, what are you going to do about it?"

RULE 7: THESE RULES MUST BECOME THE DEFINING PRINCIPLES OF YOUR LIFE.

The afternoon had faded to evening, and Jack and I were still sitting in my office when we noticed people at The Academy were heading for the doors. I needed to leave soon, but didn't want to rush Jack out of my office. We still hadn't discussed Rule 7.

"I should probably get going," Jack said. "It's late. Although you said there were seven rules, and we've only talked about six. Do we have time to finish with the seventh?"

"Of course," I answered.

"Rule 7 puts the other six into context, by essentially integrating them into one rule, rather than six separate rules.

"Rule 7 says that for these rules to have any meaning, they must become the defining principles of your life. Not *my* rules, mind you, but your rules. The rules you establish for yourself after investigating and probing into your true nature and identifying your purpose. The rules are meant to serve your aim. And for them to do so, you must accept them as a defining principle in your life. Only the Emperor inside you can do that. Not the Manager. Not the Technician. The Emperor is the one who must finally make the decision to embrace that ultimately immutable self that in one moment in time will not only find itself but be itself, and with such stunning clarity that there will be no doubt about your purpose, about your aim, about your resolution, about your Vision. At that moment you will have *become* your Vision, you will have known the truth."

"Wow," Jack said. "It's hard to imagine that kind of clarity."

"It is up to each and every one of us as Managers to create a personal bond with our own inviolable rules. Not values. Values are far too soft for what I'm talking about here. Values are passive. Rules are active. Rules penetrate every thought we have. They are self-commandments. They are invasive. They call into question every act, or every lack of act, we are given to during the course of every day. So it is that they become our defining principles, the force that pulls us back to our own chosen center. Our own chosen path. Our own duly elected way of being. They become the one and only way we can hold ourselves accountable for anything. And without that, without personal accountability, how can we expect to hold fast to any path, let alone one as difficult and as potentially rewarding as the one I'm describing? We can't."

Jack and I lingered a while longer in my office, coming down from the intense conversation we had just had. It was strange to think about how much I now knew about this man, whom I'd known so little about only a day before. It was also troubling to me to learn that someone like Jack, so full of talent and passion, was floundering in my very own organization.

Later, at home, Ilene and the kids long since asleep, I sat alone over a glass of wine, thinking about Jack, The Academy, and the seven rules. "What are *your* rules?" I thought to myself. The seven would have to do for now. As I walked down the stairs from my office to our bedroom, I looked forward to shepherding Jack through the self-discovery of becoming an E-Myth Manager.

4

THE EMPEROR, THE MANAGER,
AND THE TECHNICIAN

Where people once sought information to manage the real contexts of their lives, now they had to invent contexts in which otherwise useful information might be put to some apparent use.

Neil Postman, Amusing Ourselves to Death: Public Discourse in the Age of Show Business

I arrived at the office earlier than usual the day after my conversation with Jack. It was true that I was excited about the dialogue we had started—but I was also a little concerned about Jack. Becoming an E-

Myth Manager is a process, for sure, and most of my clients receive the information first in digestible chunks—through my tapes, my seminars, or a book like this—long before they are ever actually engaged in the process of translating it into action. Poor Jack had gotten the crash course all in one day!

I was thinking about this when I entered the lobby and saw Jack already there. He looked sort of awful, his hair sticking up every which way, and his complexion a grayish, pasty pallor. I was sure our talk had driven him to the edge.

"God, Jack, what happened to you?" I asked, not sure I wanted to know.

"The E-Myth Manager has happened to me!" he shouted, jubilant. Clearly, he'd gone mad.

"I have been up all night, thinking about what we talked about. And you're right—you're so right! I have been sleepwalking since I was a teenager, and I hadn't even noticed. In my job, in my relationships, in my life. I kept going over things in my head last night, realizing that if I don't change now, my life will be over and I won't even have noticed!"

"That's great, Jack," I offered, though he was scaring me a little with his intensity. "Just don't think you can overhaul your life all at once. In our E-Myth Mastery Program, I have begun to teach Managers how to make the transition from where they are to revolutionizing their organization, which of course begins with them personally—and we'll get to that. But there's a lot more you need to know about the nature of work before you can begin to do that work."

"So what are we waiting for?!" Jack shouted as he ran into my office.

*　　*　　*

I had my assistant cancel my meetings for the day, realizing Jack was in need of attention. I set him up with some breakfast, and we began.

"So, how to begin all over again? This is the question every Manager must ask himself. For if what I say is true, and my work with thousands of Managers confirms it, the organizations within which Managers find themselves today are consumed by personal aims that have little if anything to do with the Managers who are expected to fulfill them. Today's organization is filled with empty missions, no matter how grand and challenging and *contemporary* they might sound, or how truly important they might seem in the short term. The fact is, no self-respecting human would put 'He Nursed the Internet into Being (1981-2025)' on his gravestone. Clearly, something must be done if the Manager is to find meaning.

"The rules are a start. They provide a foundation. But once we accept them, we have to focus our attention on the organization itself for the rules to make any pragmatic sense. We must then build a new relationship with the responsibilities and accountabilities we have been given. With the people with whom we work, and for whom we work. We must undertake a wholesale reinvention of what it means to be a Manager, now that we have discovered the utter need, and possibility, of finding meaning and freedom in what we do.

THE ORGANIZATION OF WORK

"Before you can launch full-force into transforming your life and work, Jack, you need to develop a better understanding of the nature of work.

"The organization of work is best looked at much as we looked at ourselves as three distinct internal personalities with three distinct accountabilities: the Emperor, the Manager, and the Technician.

"In the organization of work, the three divisions are defined best as the enterprise, the business, and the practice; with the Emperor obviously focused on the enterprise, the Manager on the business, and the Technician on the practice.

"As I say this, Jack, it's important for you to understand that when we speak here of the organization of work, we're not speaking of the organization at large, but of *your* organization, the one for which you are accountable and the one over which you should have some measure of authority.

"And herein lies the primary focus in reinventing the work that you do: if you have accountability, but lack the clearly defined authority to implement it, you must get the authority you need or the game's over before it begins. This is absolutely essential. Without the authority, there can be no accountability."

"I know that," Jack offered.

"I know that you know that, Jack—what Manager doesn't? I also know that if you are like most Managers I have known, you condone the withholding of authority from you more often than you would care to admit. But in so doing, you create an impasse impossible to overcome.

"Without the authority you need to fulfill your accountability—*as you perceive it*—you have been rendered invisible and impotent by the powers that be. And in reality, while *they* wielded the ax, in most cases I have witnessed, it is the Manager who put his own head on the chopping block. Whether the ax falls or not, that Manager has become what I call a diminished Manager. A diminished Manager is one who lives in a world of diminished capability. In such a world most, if not all, authority is given up. And because most authority is given up, a diminished Manager has also relinquished his need to take responsibility for anything. If the ax falls it falls. Oh, of course, if things work out the Manager will take credit for it. Who wouldn't? But if things don't, and they most often don't—how *could* they under these circumstances?—it's invariably someone else's fault.

"Accountability without authority *feels* safer—that's why we agree to it. But that guise of security is what best defines the Manager's trap. If you accept accountability with diminished authority, no matter how seemingly comfortable, the inevitable sleep begins. The sleep of waiting for something, *anything* to happen. The sleep of the tyranny of routine. The sleep of diminished capacity, of diminished capability, but most of all, the sleep of diminished interest."

"It's awful to admit it to you, but it's true," Jack answered.

"Confront these questions squarely, Jack. They are critical to your life and livelihood. They will reveal you to yourself. They will help you to understand your malaise, your cynicism, your intolerance for the 'system.' They will show you how you and the people who work for you can coerce one another into simply putting in your time without a thought about what that time really means; and how, by giving it up, inch by inch, minute by minute, you have, in fact, given up your life, bit by bit by bit.

"So, Jack, in order to transform your work as a Manager, you must secure the authority necessary to fulfill your accountabilities."

"I have the authority at The Academy . . . I think," Jack responded. His doubt began to show itself in his face.

"You *may* think you already have it. But in the spirit of Rule 5, I'm asking you to question that. Because as we proceed to reinvent your work as a Manager, you're going to discover that a great deal of authority is needed that you don't have, that you have never had, because you have never really wanted it. But now, if the process we're going to engage in together is to work, you will absolutely need to find the courage to accept your own authority.

AND HERE'S THE HARD PART

"If you can't get the authority you need, *get out of here!*

"That's right, Jack. I'm telling you that if you can't get the authority you need at The Academy, get out of here. And do it fast. Because without the authority, there can be no reinvention, there can be no improvement, there can be no independence, there can be no evolution. There can be no rules. There can be no game worth playing. There can be no risk. There can be no innovation. There can be no creativity. There can be no understanding. There can be no freedom. There can be no love.

"But *with* the authority," I continued, "we can first begin to play the game in earnest.

"So let me explain how it works."

The Enterprise, the Business, the Practice

"Authority, Jack, comes in several forms—the authority of the Emperor, the authority of the Manager, and the authority of the Technician.

"Remember, when we speak of these three roles, we're describing you, the one person you believe yourself to be, acting out your relationship with yourself and the organization of which you are a part, through these three distinctly unique internal personalities, or points of view.

"The Emperor has the authority to decide the direction of the enterprise. What the focus of the enterprise must be. Where the enterprise will ultimately be positioned in the world—which is to say, in the minds of those people with whom it interacts: its

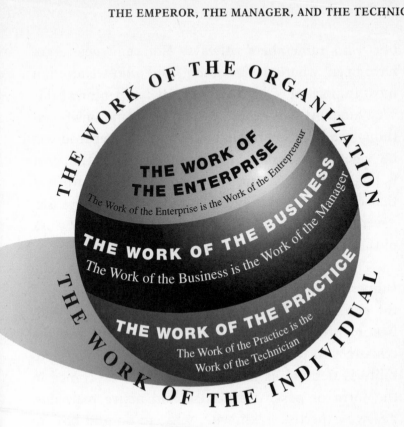

THE WORK OF THE ORGANIZATION

THE WORK OF THE ENTERPRISE
The Work of the Enterprise is the Work of the Entrepreneur

THE WORK OF THE BUSINESS
The Work of the Business is the Work of the Manager

THE WORK OF THE PRACTICE
The Work of the Practice is the Work of the Technician

THE WORK OF THE INDIVIDUAL

customers, its employees, its suppliers, its lenders—and how it will accomplish that hopefully unique and highly differentiated position. The Emperor provides not only the direction for the Manager and the Technician, but the will and *wakefulness* necessary to remember it. If forgetting our aim and who we are in this moment is what defines the tragedy of man—and it is—then the Emperor should be thought of as the one who remembers. Always. Not only where we have been, where we are going, and who we are, but most important of all, what is truly happening at this very moment. So if there can be an Emperor of any-thing—and I'm saying there always has been and will be, whether we create him or not—then our Emperor is the Emperor of truth. And our Emperor's truth is that there will be an enterprise within which we dis-cover our selves while simultaneously doing the work of the world.

"The Manager has the authority to manifest the Emperor's Vision in the operation of the business of the enterprise. The Manager has three accountabili-ties: to provide the capability, the capacity, and the resources for the enterprise to fulfill its Vision. Capa-bility is defined as know-how. Know-how comes in the form of passive expertise and active expertise. Passive expertise is knowing what to do and how to do it, and where that is absent, finding out how. Active expertise is the skill that transforms passive expertise into action. Active expertise manifests itself in the form of processes and systems. One of the Manager's primary accountabilities is to invent such processes and systems. Once processes and systems are invented and implemented, the Manager's pri-mary accountability is to monitor their effectiveness. The effectiveness of a system or process is judged by its ability to mirror the Emperor's Vision exactly. If *exactly* is a 10, then anything less than a 10 calls for improvement. Passive expertise is in a continuous dialogue with active expertise to discover the models for improvement, the continuous process of reinventing the processes and systems called innovation. The Manager monitors this process as well, and has the authority and resources required to implement whatever is discovered and decided there to reinvent existing processes and systems as they are called for.

"The Technician has the authority to exercise her capability, capacity, and resources to implement the Manager's processes and systems to fulfill the Emperor's Vision. The Technician is either an apprentice, a craftsman, or a master. Whichever her designation may be, the resident capabilities, capacities, and resources that define the role she is presently fulfilling provide the objective measure for the Technician's continuous process of personal and operational improvement at that level. Both the Emperor and the Manager understand only too well that without the Technician's dedication to this process of improvement, the entire enterprise would come crashing down, its higher purpose unsustainable. That is why the level within the hierarchy where every Technician plays out his or her role is called the practice. Because that is what the Technician does—practice. Indeed, the Technician never grows beyond practice. It is the rule that defines her existence. Whether the Technician is an apprentice, a craftsman, or a master, the practice is always there, always beyond reach, always calling the Technician forward.

"Were it not for the Emperor, the Technician would forget why she is doing this thing called practice, or even *that* she is doing it. For the Technician who forgets, practice can become the work I do, rather than the work I practice.

"Were it not for the Manager, the Technician would not realize that all practice reveals itself as a process, or as a system. There is a system of practice, a process through which results are produced. The Manager translates the Emperor's Vision into the practical stuff that every Technician needs to know for her own personal satisfaction, for her own personal methodology for growth.

"Were it not for the Emperor and the Manager, the Technician would get lost in routine, in chisels and hammers and software and all of the other distracting realities of a Technician's world. The Emperor invents a church to serve God. This is the enterprise. The Manager defines the best way to build the church, assembles the resources, the people, the expertise, the plans. This is the business. The Technician shapes the stones and moves them into place.

This is the practice. The church begins its journey upward.

THE DISCRIMINATING MANAGER

"So the work of every Manager falls into three categories: the Emperor's work, the Manager's work, the Technician's work. Every Manager must learn the differences among these three, and the role each must come to play in the organization if he is to lead a balanced, productive existence. In short, each and every Manager must learn to discriminate between the appropriate type of work to be done at any one moment, as well as to formulate an ideal relationship among the three forms of work in the development of oneself as an effective Manager.

"There is no exact formula for this. The formula is determined for every one of us depending upon our naturally habituated fixation.

"Some Managers find it virtually impossible to en*vision* anything other than the job at hand. Work beckons them wherever they look. Work is a drug that transfixes them to the workbench, to the computer, to the cell phone, to the people in their organization, to the customer, to the Internet, to endless meetings with other Managers. In short, most Managers are fixated at the Technician's level, despite the fact that they supposedly left that work behind when they first became a Manager.

"To such Managers, the work is endless in both variety and number. And naturally, if work is endless and if work is one's fixation, we find it, always, and do it, always, with nervous, often brash, sometimes unreasonably angry, intensity. Are you a Manager like that? Do you find yourself stepping in to do the Technician's work continually out of a belief that no one will ever do it as well as you? Do you realize as you do this the price you are paying for your compulsion to hold on to the Technician's role, despite the fact that you have already elected to move out of it? Clearly, what you find yourself in is not a practice— there is no improvement going on here—but doing work for work's sake. Chisel the stone, chisel the stone. But what of God? Or what of the church? Or what of the strategy for building the church? Or what of the lessons to be learned as an apprentice, a craftsman, a master? And what is mastery, after all?

"In most organizations such questions not only go unasked, but if asked are immediately and summarily put to rest.

"In most organizations there is no God, there is no church, there is no higher aim. There is only survival, and the Emperor's passion. Which is the Emperor's outsized need. Which, as we've already said, becomes the theme of communication throughout the organization at large.

"Such organizations, as every Manager reading this book knows, can be a living death. But not always. There is also the excitement such organizations can create when things are going well. Which means, in the Emperor's language, when the Vision seems to be coming to life. In such organizations, greed and its traveling companion, fear, fill the halls and cubicles. In such organizations, passion is a big word. A defining principle. A measure of a person's commitment. In such organizations, Managers are *expected* to act like Technicians. Management is a stage, not a commitment. In such organizations, you can wear the title of Manager and never do management work at all. As long as the results are being produced, no one really cares.

"But to the *Manager* who cares, a huge price is being paid. Because to the Manager who cares, management is not a stage, but a commitment to personal growth.

"If a Manager's fixation is to do the work of the Technician, there is only one path to take. Stop. Do no technical work at all. When the phone rings, have someone else answer it. When the software breaks down, have someone else fix it. When a customer comes in, have someone else take care of her. When the Managers call a meeting, find a reason to be someplace else, anyplace else. Replace your compulsion to do with a compulsion to be. Begin the process of discovery into the nature of Emperor work. Begin with these questions: What do I want? What is the enterprise I'm inventing here? What is its purpose? Sit down with a blank pad and think about ends rather than means. Go away from where the work is being done. Go away from the business. Go to a park. Go to a movie. Go home. Go anywhere but where you are. Every Manager needs to do this for herself every so often. Work is seductive, and we've been conditioned to fall hard. Work provides us with an undeniably satisfying experience of producing something worthwhile. Thinking doesn't do that. At least, not at the beginning it doesn't. Thinking can be regarded as a complete waste of time. Especially by the resident Technician who is just aching to be busy.

"On the other hand, there are those Managers who are fixated on dreaming. For whom the 'big picture' is intoxicating. For whom planning or en*visioning* is a perpetual state, rather than one that will be implemented. For such Managers, there is always the rush to the 'big idea,' which is most often a rush *away* from the 'little idea,' the idea of work. I call such a person the Emperor with no purpose. It's the bogus

Emperor I spoke about earlier. It's the attraction to the never-ending flow of ideas, ideas without legs or feet. Ideas that will never walk in the world. To such a Manager, the strategy is clear. Take any single idea and put it to work. Put it to work yourself. Go through the painful process of trying to manifest the idea in reality. Make the calls necessary. Write the manual, and then follow its prescriptions. Add up the numbers, and then test them against reality. Do whatever the idea needs you to do to become a result, or to prove that it wasn't such a good idea after all. Until a Manager sees through his ideas a sufficient number of times to taste the process through which an idea is born, expanded upon, organized into a process or system, implemented, monitored, improved upon, and then either kept or dropped as a working part of the organization, there can be no understanding or appreciation for how much of a commitment and how much energy ideas can consume from everyone in the organization.

"Then there are the Managers who just *love* to manage. They think of themselves as 'people persons.' You know them. They spend an inordinate amount of their time and ours talking to their people or anyone who will listen. They are forever in meetings, behind closed doors, conferring in serious tones about the personal challenges and opportunities their people are either failing to address, or if they are addressing them, failing to appreciate. There are so many subtleties appreciated by people persons that the rest of us fail to notice. People persons are on a mission from God. They would have us all believe that their insights and their passion for the human condition, and their enthusiastic, selfless contribution to its transformation, is what management is all about. It is not. As we will learn later on in this book, in the most enlightened organizations, Managers do not manage people, people manage themselves. In such organizations, the people person will quickly, and abruptly, come face to face with his fixation, which is to attempt to create in relationship with others that which does not exist in himself, namely, relationship. The job, then, for any Manager who recognizes himself in this description is to quit schmoozing immediately. Pretend that you have been prohibited from ever consulting with your people again, but that you must produce results through these people. How would you do it? What options are left? At first, facing the gloom of no schmoozing, every people person you know will immediately fall into deep depression. If not that, then what? What's life all about but schmoozing with people? What does a Manager do, if not that? And then gradually, if a Manager is committed to the process I'm recommending here, options will begin to flower like a cherry tree in spring. Soon the work of a Manager, and the opportunities it presents to the mind and the heart, will begin to reveal themselves in diverse and intelligent splendor. Eventually, the energy that has been committed to the people-person persona—and wasted there in useless chatter—will be expanded to discover whole new ways of working, entirely new dimensions of the Manager's own spirit and imagination, and a healthy new respect for his people's ability to take on the responsibility of managing themselves, while practicing new processes and systems.

*   *   *

"So you see, discrimination is the process of choice, Jack. To choose, one must have standards. To have standards, one must have a Vision. And to have a Vision, one must rise above the whole organization to see its place in the world. And to see the organization's place in the world, one must have the ability to rise above oneself, to see one's place in the world, in relationship to the organization, as well as outside of it. And to rise above oneself, one must possess the ability to focus one's attention in an uncommon way. And to develop such an attention one must practice, practice, practice. That is the work of an E-Myth Manager."

"Great!" Jack said. "When can I begin?"

5

RECONCILING THE VISION

. . . anybody who wants anything need only do the work.

Swami Chetanananda, **Dynamic Stillness**

Two weeks had passed since the meeting with Jack in my office, and he called to ask if we could meet. He had been thinking about little else since our conversation, he told me, and wanted to ask me some questions and share some of his thoughts with me. We arranged to meet at my home office.

It was a stormy day in late November. From my home office I could see the Sonoma hills, which were fast becoming a carpet of green as they do every winter. The pouring rain and the green hills served as a counterpoint to the red and orange flames of the fire I had just built in my fireplace. Jack hung up his wet coat and sat down in front of the fire, rubbing his hands vigorously to dispel the cold. His eyes glowed with intensity. He began to speak.

"First of all, I want to tell you how much our conversations have meant to me," Jack said. "Thinking about the organization in that way made me think about my relationship to work. You took me back to my days at Stanford, when questioning, for me, was a way of life. It was exciting and intoxicating to think and to challenge myself, my professors, other students. I remember feeling like I was pursuing the most serious questions one could in life, and that it was not only all right to do so, but that it was the reason I was there! It really made me feel alive.

"And then, for whatever reason, I sort of left that mentality behind when I took my first career position. It was as if the world of work was the real world and the world of school had just been theory, child's play, an extended word problem or debate.

"At least, that's how my first Manager spoke of our relationship on my first day. He told me, 'This is the *real* world, Jack, this isn't school. So watch me closely,' he said, 'watch what I do, and then *do* it. I don't have time to nurse you along. You're going to have to figure out things for yourself. But if you watch me,' he said, 'you'll get it. And if you don't'. . . He shrugged then," Jack said, "and what I knew as certainly as I knew anything was that that shrug meant that if I *didn't* get it, I was gone."

Jack went on, "I had no idea what he was talking about! 'Get *what?*' I thought to myself. What was this mysterious, indescribable thing my Manager was going to do that I had to get by simply watching him? How would I even *recognize* it, if *he* couldn't—or wouldn't—describe it to me?

"Well, it didn't take me long to figure it out. *There really wasn't any mystery to it at all*. What my Manager was really saying to me was that when he needed something, I was the one who was going to get it. And mostly what he needed were answers. Answers to questions other people were always asking him, or about to ask him, but which he himself didn't have the answers to."

Jack continued, "Understand, that didn't stop my Manager from *giving* answers to questions he didn't know the answers to. He did that all the time. I was astonished. How could a serious Manager in a serious company build his credibility on answers that were complete, unadulterated bullshit?

"I swear, this is true," Jack said. "What I learned during those first few years of my career was that most of the people I reported to knew little or nothing about the solutions they were providing to their Managers, their people, or our customers. It came to be the joke around the office. I swear, the lesson my Manager wanted me to learn was that it didn't *matter* what you said one day, you could completely change your tune the very next . . . *and no one would even notice!*

"But of course, you could only go so far with bull-shit. Ultimately, you needed to have an answer. And that was my job: to find answers when they were absolutely needed.

"My job was to always make sure the boss, my Manager, looked good. And until you and I started talking a few weeks ago, no one I had ever worked for had done anything other than support that belief. I always got ahead at work by showing up with the answers to somebody else's questions; and if I didn't have the answers, I'd make certain I found them before anyone else did.

"In fact, since I joined The E-Myth Academy, I've been doing that here. And it's always gotten me good grades. Nobody ever told me that I wasn't supposed to make the boss look good, because whenever I did it, everyone seemed to acknowledge me for it.

"So when we started talking at dinner, I was truly surprised by what you said. I've been trying to recon-cile the picture I've had of what I *believed* you wanted from me at work with the picture you painted for me. And they didn't seem to mesh."

"They don't," I answered. "But not for the reasons you think.

"Your first Manager is what I call the diminished Manager. All he was really doing with *you* is what someone else did with *him*. That's the politics of the Emperor's organization. Everything rolls downhill, and the guy at the bottom who's trying to climb up the hill is expected to catch it. That's the deal. Catch it, or fail. You are not going to get to the top of the hill any other way. The shrewd guy at the bottom of the hill begins very early on to understand the rules of the Emperor's game.

"Understand, Jack, no matter what anybody tells you, and no matter how things seem to the contrary, the game of every organization *always* starts at the top, not somewhere in the middle. There are no exceptions to this. The Manager you just described to me honestly believed what he was telling you. In his mind, he was giving you good advice, the only advice he *could* give you under the circumstances; because it's what he learned how to do to get where he was in the organization. I can absolutely promise you that his first Manager—and then the one after that, and the one after that—said, 'Watch me. And do what I do.' Whether it was actually said or simply implied, it was communicated to him nonetheless. And they said it because that's what the Emperor was saying, and is saying, in every Emperor-led organization. 'Watch me, and do what I do.' That mind-set rolls down from the Emperor to the next Manager in line, and then to the next Manager, and so on until it reaches everyone else in the organization, all of the people looking up to them. Which of course is where the conversation about management stops. Which is what happens between Managers and those who report to them: the conversation stops. Which is to say that there can be no communication between a Manager and his or her people about the mystery called management that proposes, Watch Me, and do what I do.

"And so, to those non-Managers radiating throughout the organization, those people I call Technicians doing what Technicians are supposed to do in any organization—make stuff, sell stuff, automate stuff, administer stuff—the mystery of management isn't what *you* were led to believe it to be. The mystery of management to every Technician in every organization around the world is that it works *at all!*

"To everyone other than the Managers, management is a secret society within which there are invisible, seemingly illogical, rules. To the Technician who is not attracted to becoming a Manager, these rules are seen for what they actually are—absolutely insane.

"But when you *join* that society, when you are *attracted* to that game, like you've always been, when you are motivated to climb the organizational hill, you are first introduced to a game that is by now so thickly encrusted with the cynicism that comes from knowing, in everything you are expected to do, that management has nothing to do with how much you know, or how truthful you are, or how direct your communication is, but exactly the opposite. The management game as it's played in most organizations has only to do with how well you play it. Are you a player, or aren't you? If you are, you are shrewd enough to understand the implied as well as the explicit rules of the game, which are 1) making the boss look *good* is never enough, and 2) making the boss look *great* is what a true player learns to do. You need to make the diminished Manager look great to *himself*. Fail at that, and it doesn't matter how great a job you've done for him; he will never forgive you."

"You're telling me," said Jack. "That's exactly how it was at my last job."

"So it becomes immediately obvious to someone like you, Jack, just leaving school and walking into the 'real world,' that the 'real world,' the world of work, the world of your father and your mother, and of their fathers, is the place where, if we are attracted to rising in the organization, we are expected to give up childish pursuits. Like thinking. Like questioning. Like telling the truth, being honest, and doing your homework. In short, everything and anything you were supposed to do in school, everything that was supposed to shape you as a child, give you your moral and ethical underpinnings, all of that in the 'real world' is thought of as counterproductive, childish pursuits. Instead, they say, let's get down to business."

*   *   *

Jack and I took a break. The rain had stopped and the sun was shining, so we decided to walk around outside. The air was crisp. We walked over to the koi pond I had built over the summer. The koi were, as always, a joy to watch, their gold and black and orange and white reflections shining back at the sun through the clear, cold water. The lily pads, green and passive, moved gently with the undulating current. The pond was everything I had hoped it would be when I had conceived the idea of it more than a year before. The truth is, I knew nothing about such things. About fish and ponds and water plants. About the ecological balance that needed to be considered in the planning of it. But I had a love for them. Having such a pond had been a dream of mine for years—perhaps my own personal pyramid of sorts. I could see it in my mind's eye, just as I described it above, but I had no idea what it would take to create such a thing. As it turned out, it took a great deal more than I had ever imagined it would. The liner for the pond, the stonework around it, the filtration system and pump that made it possible for the whole thing to work; all of that took more time—and much more money—than I, or the people who were building it for me, had projected.

But why should I have expected the construction of a pond to be different from the construction of my business? Of course, it could be argued that the pond was much simpler. The knowns were more easily known. The unknowns less problematic. But in reality, that wasn't true. In reality, everything came as a surprise to everyone who should not have been surprised. After all, weren't the people I had contracted to build the pond experts in the process? I thought they were. And candidly, so did they. They had built ponds before. They understood liners and stone and filters and fish. But nothing worked out as it was supposed to. They were indeed experts, and they still are experts, but something essential was missing. And that was what Jack and I were discussing. The expertise that was missing in the men I had hired to build the pond was the expertise of a Manager.

We went back up to my office, and continued our conversation.

*   *   *

Jack was having trouble understanding how he could both take to heart the advice I'd given him—something he clearly wanted to do—and at the same time, continue to work and be successful at The E-Myth Academy, where he would ostensibly make my Vision, as Emperor, his second priority. It seemed clear to me that the problem was the way Jack was thinking about the two goals—as opposites.

I decided to walk him through both philosophies, step by step.

"Let's talk about what you believe my expectation is for you at work. You believe that I expect you to implement my Vision. And in order to do that responsibly you need to make it yours. In other words, you think I want you to be an E-Myth true believer. And if you were an E-Myth true believer, you would do whatever it takes to make my Vision a reality. In short, Jack, you think I want you to make me look good by making my Vision a reality. Right?"

"Yes," he said, his cheeks flushing. He was obviously embarrassed by the picture I created. And who wouldn't be? It was such a narcissistic perspective. Who would want to admit such a thing? First, that I *wanted* him to behave that way, and second, that he would *agree* to behave that way. Was this the deal we had unwittingly made with each other when he had come to work for the company?

"Okay, then, let's look at the second point of view, the one I shared with you a few weeks ago.

"The second point of view is represented by the seven rules. But rather than repeat them, let's integrate them into one essential idea: that it is a Manager's sole accountability to serve himself, or to put it more effectively, to become his own Emporer.

"That what *I* want from our relationship must always be secondary to what *you* want from our relationship. And that if it isn't, what I want will ultimately cost you your freedom.

"The conflict between those two points of view becomes obvious, if in fact they are as we've stated. The conflict is between what I want and what you want. If your job is to give me what I want, then it stands to reason that what you want is irrelevant unless it is the same as what I want. Does that make sense, Jack?" I asked him.

"Yes, it seems to," he answered.

"Let me show you where the contradiction lies. While it is your belief that I want you to be a true believer in the E-Myth Point of View, nothing could be further from the truth.

"What I *actually* want from you is a commitment

to decide what it is that *you* believe, completely apart from what I believe.

"Because until you do that, you haven't made nearly as deep a commitment to our relationship as I have. Before ever meeting you Jack, I spent years thinking about and pondering one question: What is a business and how does one work?

"And only after spending all those years thinking about it and talking, talking, talking to Managers and executives and small-business owners and Technicians did I come to an understanding of the condition that exists in most businesses. My conclusions are what I write about in my books and what I collectively call the E-Myth Point of View. I communicate that point of view to everyone I come into contact with, every chance I get: prospective employees, old employees, prospective clients, existing clients, as well as audiences throughout the world.

"And what happens when I do that is that people take these conclusions, and agree with them, argue with them, laugh at them, cry because of them; just about anything you could possibly imagine happens when I share this point of view with people who are for their own reasons interested in business."

"Just as I did when I forced my way into your office that day," he smiled.

"With *The E-Myth*, my first book, the audience is

the owner or prospective owner of a business, because that's who the book was written for. But it's also essential that anyone who comes to work here at The E-Myth Academy take whatever time is necessary to come to grips with the E-Myth Point of View, and challenge it to their heart's content, either on their own, or directly with me, or with anyone else they care to talk to at The Academy.

"Because if they don't, and they come to work here, they will ultimately be forced to make a decision. A decision about whether or not they can fully commit themselves to a company that professes with all its heart the point of view I've committed myself to.

"So, Jack, it is not that I want you to be a true believer in the E-Myth. Not at all. What I *do* want is for you to decide in your own mind and in your own heart how you feel about the subject the E-Myth addresses, whether or not you agree with my perspective on the plight of most businesses, and that you wrestle with the same subjects that I did. Only *after* that inquiry, and only *after* you've decided for yourself whether or not you are determined, for your very own reasons, to bring this message to the world, only then—and I mean this—only then can we work together as equals, each dedicated to pursuing this Vision as differentiated individuals, each on his own path in life. If not, we should part company before we each begin to blame the other for feeling let down."

Jack looked down at the floor.

"And, should we decide to work together toward this end, then, and only then, must you begin the process by constructing a view of your own organization, independent of me, to show me how you can add value here.

"So you see that these are not contradictory points of view at all, but actually one and the same. My point of view is critical for you to understand before we come to work together, because it is the point of view that has created this organization and to which the organization is committed. But until you define your own point of view, your own Vision, until you can create your own rules and answer your own questions as I feel I have answered mine, only then can we come to agreement or not."

Jack nodded in understanding.

"Then, and only then, what's left for us to do here is to go one step further to discuss how you would begin the reinvention of your work at The Academy now that we are agreed in our commitment to our shared Vision.

*   *   *

"If an organization's mind-set is shaped from the top down—and it undeniably is—then the Manager's organization must be shaped in the very same way. Whether the organization is made up of three people or four hundred, whether it is a sales group or a manufacturing group, if the organization is led by a Manager, that Manager has not only the opportunity but the obligation to shape its mind-set; but not the way it has traditionally been done in most organizations. In the Manager's organization, the mantra is not 'Watch me and do what I do,' but rather 'Forget about me and let's see what *it* does.' *It* being the organization. What's it supposed to be doing? What's it actually doing? What's happening at the enterprise, at the business, at the practice levels of the organization? How do these three play out in their relationships with each other? If there is one result more important than all the rest that we're accountable for, what is it? How good are we at producing that result? How bad? What beliefs do my people have about management, about work, about their jobs specifically, about the way results are produced in the organization generally, about their compensation, about their future in the organization, and after they leave the organization, about trust, about commitment, about clear communication, about our integrity, about the processes and systems we use to produce results, and more? What beliefs do our customers have about how well or how badly we keep our promises? Do we even make promises? If so, what are they? How do we know when we keep them? How do we act on what we know? Do we have a system for acting on what we know? Do we have a system for creating a system when we don't have one?

"At the heart of reinventing the Manager's organization is your accountability to put everything you believe to be true, believe needs to be true, everything you want to be true, or are not certain is true into serious question. In short, you need to discover what *is* true about your organization. That's the baseline in the process. Stripping the organization down to its essential truth. So you and your people can look at it exactly as it is, rather than how you both imagine it to be. In the reinvention of your organization, imagination can be a deadly thing.

"The second part of the process is to ask yourself what other organizations within your company are accountable for, which of those are accountable to your organization, and which of those is your organization accountable to. And as you begin that process, you will begin to see a map emerging, which defines conduits of transactions, interactions, and input of information, products, services, capital, and resources, plus expertise and people, all of it flowing in multiple directions throughout the organization and around the organization proper. A moving matrix of activity and intelligence, processes and systems, beginnings and ends, products, services, and people, all working very hard, or not at all, or somewhere in between, to produce some semblance of a consistent result that defines ultimately—or, better stated, ideally *should* define—the singular product the larger organization has promised to deliver to its world of customers. I call that singular product the differentiated product, which every company should be determined to define first, and then artfully produce, consistently and predictably time after time.

"Having identified these other organizations—I'll call them peer organizations—within the organization at large, your next step is to do the same thing with the Managers of those organizations that you've done with your own. To discover the truth about them.

"This, of course, is easier said than done. Most Managers aren't interested in the truth; the truth can be dangerous because if it is a truth you don't want to hear, you're then stuck with the fact of it. Once it's out of the bag there's no putting it back in again. The other catch about the truth is that once it's out you have to *do* something about it. That is more than most Managers can handle. Given the inordinate amount of technical work each is doing, there is little time left in the day for engaging in this type of Managerial work.

"So how does Jack engage his peers in what is on the face of it a 'Come to Jesus' meeting about the truth? We'll deal with this question in Part 2 of the book, but know that it is a question every Manager needs to ask in order to move his organization from where it is, in its present old-world mind-set, to where it could be. The purpose of the process is to enable you to discover what's true about your business, and how you as a Manager can effectively transform your relationship with both the organization you are accountable for and the organization that has hired you to do this job. The purpose of this process is also to enable you to understand how you can turn what has been engineered as a dependent, controlled, manipulated role in someone else's company into an independent, extraordinarily freeing role that will teach you how to make wherever you are fulfilling this management accountability you hold so dear an enterprise of your own."

*   *   *

"So, Jack," I said to him. "The end point of this conversation we're having is this: if I can expect anything of you working at The Academy, it is to develop in you the need for your own enterprise, and the skills with which to accomplish it. This should be every Emperor's aim, but in many cases, it is not. So it must be the Manager's aim. Each and every Manager in each and every organization must come to agreement within himself that the primary purpose of the job he's got is to prepare himself for the next one. A better, bigger, more important job. Yet what if such a job didn't exist? What if, after twenty-two years of work, you had to begin all over again, as so many have before and so many will again in the future? Or what if, after pleasing the Emperor for so many years, you finally came to the grand conclusion that it was high time to go to work for yourself? Yet at that point, where you're making one of the most significant decisions of your working life, you come to realize that none of the companies you've worked for equipped you with the full set of skills you'd need to thrive outside of that organization? You realize that you spent so many valuable years rushing to exact the Emperor's will, realize his dream, make him look good—with no lasting payback, no authority to pursue your own goals, no accountability for your own organization, much less yourself? The truth is, Jack, few Managers are truly prepared, emotionally, intellectually or financially, to build an enterprise of their own without the resources of the organizations they have worked in all of their lives.

"That's what becoming an E-Myth Manager is all about. The E-Myth Manager is one who understands the temporary nature of management work. To the E-Myth Manager, management is a benchmark in a life-transforming process. It is the benchmark between the work of the Technician and the work of the Emperor, or what I call the work of the Entrepreneur. Whether or not the Manager is ever willing to create an actual enterprise of her own isn't so much the point; the goal is to reinvent the Manager's role and mind-set in an entrepreneurial way to bring greater authority, conviction, accountability, productivity, and yes, happiness to her life. But without meaning there can be no happiness. So the entire process I'm describing is one of continuing wakefulness. Because until one has developed the awareness, the sensitivity, the sensibilities, the skills, and the know-how necessary to the process of inventing and growing one's own enterprise, she is in fact only a shadow of the Manager who could truly contribute to her organization's vitality, growth, and success.

"Show me an organization in which the critical focus is developing Managers with passion and objectivity, and I will show you an organization that is not only fully alive itself, but that is a force field for the birth of countless extraordinary ventures that themselves will multiply and flourish.

"Can you see the power of such an idea, Jack? Can

you see both the emotional and the economic impact of such a thing?"

Jack nodded his head, his eyes bright and alert.

"The next step is to talk about how to do that," I said.

Let's get on with it.

PART 2

BUILDING THE
ENTREPRENEURIAL
ORGANIZATION

6

GETTING STARTED

"Do you have a definition of human purpose you would have me consider?"

"I would have you consider that the highest purpose of the human species is to justify the gift of life."

Norman Cousins, The Celebration of Life

To become an E-Myth Manager—to truly own your job, do it better than you ever have before, and derive from it the meaning and satisfaction we all crave—is to become an Entrepreneur. Which is not to say that you should begin to think about starting a business, owning a business, or leaving the job you have—although you may well do that after finishing this book. To become an E-Myth Manager, you must embark upon a process of discovery and shed the skin the organization has demanded you grow to uncover within yourself the best Manager you can and want to be.

That process must happen in two ways. Both begin with you.

The first involves redefining your relationship within yourself as it pertains to the organization. And it's important to note that when I say the *organization*, I mean *your* organization. *Your* organization consists of your department, your division, your team—the sales organization, the accounts receivable organization, the manufacturing organization, the engineering organization. The first step in becoming an E-Myth Manager is to think about this organization as if it truly were your own—an enterprise in its own right. And though this may strike you as one small step for Managerkind, it is the step through which the larger organization can be reborn.

The second part of the process involves a kind of courageousness on the part of the evolving E-Myth Manager. A willingness to embrace what becoming an Entrepreneur really means. An Entrepreneur is single-handedly accountable for creating a Vision for her company. Traditionally, this was always done by the Emperor of the company at large, and implemented by the rest of the staff—Managers included.

But it is the work of the enterprise, or the Entrepreneur, in the E-Myth Manager Program to take on that responsibility.

In addition, a Manager must create a system through which this Vision will be optimally realized. One of the overarching problems that I've encountered in large organizations and small—which undoubtedly stems back to the origins of management as we've discussed it—is the subjectivity by which people are expected to do their jobs. Most companies don't have a system. "A system!" they'd cry. "A system would force us to face the fact that there is little, if any, agreement among the powers that be as to our real Vision." Without a system, people have no objective understanding of the nature of their work and what is expected of them—save the highly personalized goals that are set for them by their immediate superiors, who we all know have their own agendas. As a result, people are forced to do the best they can, which of course varies vastly from individual to individual. Without a system, you're playing Russian roulette with your results.

And delivering results is the last great objective of the Entrepreneur. To utilize the system to produce the desired effect in pursuit of your Vision is to get results. So many companies today are so caught up in the bottom line that their entire focus is dependent upon it: cut costs, improve productivity, do better, do more, and do it faster is their mantra. Of course it is—everyone wants to make money, and it's harder than ever in today's business climate. The point they're missing in that bottom-line mentality, however, is the very key, the very essence to achieving those big numbers:

To produce more and better, and improve profits, you need to know why you're doing what your doing and you need a system through which to implement it.

To build the entrepreneurial organization, each and every entrepreneurial Manager must assume the task of creating the Vision, the system, and the results for his team. In so doing, he will create positive energy within his organization, rather than consume negativity. He will increase possibilities for his people, rather than reduce them to a state of confusion. He will help people relearn to think for themselves, to rediscover a kind of joy and pride in what they're doing—or not. In either case, his people will thank him for it, and his organization will thrive as a result. In this way, he will create abundance for everyone his organization has a relationship with—from the people who work in it to the people who buy from it. From the people who own it to the people who finance it.

This is the philosophy of the E-Myth Manager. And this is the program for realizing it.

SEVEN STEPS TO BECOMING AN E-MYTH MANAGER

There are seven steps to becoming an E-Myth Manager, and for transforming your organization. They are: your Primary Aim, your Strategic Objective, your Financial Strategy, your Organizational Strategy, your Management Strategy, your People Strategy, and your Marketing Strategy.

Understanding the nature of these seven steps and how they relate to each other is critical to your ultimate success in changing your organization, your job, your life, and the lives of the people who work for you. The balance of this book is devoted to an exploration of these steps.

A word of caution to the reader. As I've said in each of my previous books, and I'll say again: this book is not about *how* to do the work of an E-Myth Manager, it's about *what* to do. In my experience with organizations and Managers from many different industries, knowing *what* to do is significantly more important to the entrepreneurial organization than knowing *how* to do it. Once you know what to do, the how will quickly follow.

So let's get started.

7

THE E-MYTH MANAGER'S

PRIMARY AIM

Only when a man makes use of his power of self-awareness does he attain to the level of a person, to the level of freedom. At that moment he is living, not being lived.

E. F. Schumacher, A Guide for the Perplexed

To reinvent your organization, it is essential that you begin your relationship with it all over again. To do that, it is essential that you begin your relationship with *yourself* all over again, which means that it is essential to ask yourself one question, the single most important question any Manager can ask himself:

What do I want?

But 'What do I want?' is not just an *organization-*defining question, it is a *life*-defining question. And that's one of the first rules for creating your Primary Aim. You must first concern yourself with your life. The organization comes second.

Why you first, organization second? As a Manager, you know that to the degree the organization has shaped your life, you *have* no life; your life has been shaped by the Emperor's need for as long as you've been in his employ. And as long as your life is shaped by the Emperor's need, you are the product of the organization and judged against the image the organization has of a successful Manager. Your life, then, becomes the instrument through which someone *else* fulfills his passion and Vision.

This way of doing things clearly doesn't work for the Manager, much less for the organization or the Emperor.

So the first step in the process of becoming an E-Myth Manager has very little to do with the organization, your job as you've known it, or the Emperor's needs.

It has primarily to do with what you want for yourself. Apart *from* the organization, as opposed to as a part *of* the organization.

Your Job Is Not Your Life

The most common problem among Managers is that because they've let the organization shape their lives, they have no real identity beyond that which is deeply entrenched within the place where they work.

Most Managers have come to believe that what they do and where they do it is who they are.

For most Managers their career *is* their life.

Their work *is* their life.

Their financial security *is* their life.

These Managers have been very well trained.

From the E-Myth Manager's perspective, none of the above is true. Indeed, from the E-Myth Manager's perspective, your life *could* be all of these things if you so choose, but it needn't be that way. In fact, from the E-Myth Manager's perspective, if your life even remotely resembles this, your life cannot work.

At least not as well as it could.

That's why you need to create your Primary Aim.

Your Primary Aim is the Vision you have of the kind of life you would like to live.

Sure, some might say, "The kind of life I'd like to live has nothing whatsoever to do with the life I'm living, much less my job as a Manager. If I could, I'd be wealthy. I'd travel more. I'd say to hell with management altogether!"

As a matter of fact, that's just what the E-Myth Manager proposes. You see, to live a life that fulfills your own singular uniqueness is to live a life fully. With Vision. With accountability. As an enterprise. And to say, "To hell with management altogether," is to say, "The organization will serve me, as a vehicle through which I live the life I want to live. The enterprise is an extension of who I am, and my role as an E-Myth Manager is to transform this enterprise into a living reality that embodies what I want to accomplish and represent."

To become an E-Myth Manager, you must know that in order to create an organization that works in a powerfully human way, it is first essential to confront what it means to *you* to be truly human. You must know what you want in order to get it.

Yet make no mistake—in unearthing what the E-Myth Manager wants, and in turn transforming the organization, this is not a form of the Emperor's will. Because in discovering your Primary Aim, you will be uncovering the truths within yourself—passions and goals that will force you to decide whether or not the very organization you are in *can* become, for you, an entrepreneurial organization. It is impossible to effectively transform any organization into an independently profitable, productive, functional unit if one's aim is misguided or distorted. That's why we find ourselves in the state we do today.

THE PARADOX OF THE PRIMARY AIM

I know what you're thinking. Creating a Primary Aim feels like an unnatural act.

I've worked with thousands of Managers, and it always amazes me how they respond to the question "What do you want?" Many feel embarrassed because they're being asked to think in a way they never have before, a way that forces them to both separate themselves from their jobs and think of their organizations as an extension of themselves. And that's where the paradox comes in. Because in truth, management has less to do with what you do or what you manage than who you are. So as paradoxical as it may sound, a truly extraordinary Manager is more likely to be successful when asking, Who am I? and Why am I here? than when doing the work. When a Manager asks, Who am I? he's asking, What do I hope to accomplish with this organization? When he's asking, What do I want? he's asking, What is the single reason my business exists? The answers to both versions describe who he is—and what he wants—and how that will successfully differentiate his business from everyone else's.

Your Primary Aim is a statement of what you wish your life to look like when it's finally done. It is an essential question to be asked by anyone who manages or owns an enterprise of any kind.

*   *   *

"Let's talk about the E-Myth Manager's Primary Aim," I said to Jack, who had just arrived at my home on a cold and rainy Saturday morning. "Are you ready to do that?"

He nodded.

"The E-Myth Manager's Primary Aim can be thought of in two ways. As a technology, a tool that will help you clarify your personal objectives. In other words, in a completely pragmatic, career-related way.

"Or it could be thought about personally, in an effort to enhance self-awareness—not just as it relates to our careers, our jobs, our professions, our work; but as it relates to the question, What does it mean to be alive?

"The first way is much easier, of course. The second way is infinitely more difficult because it requires true seeing.

"As E. F. Schumacher argued in his most eloquent small book, *A Guide for the Perplexed*, man is a unique form of being. It is that uniqueness that gives us our possibilities. Schumacher said, 'While an animal is conscious, man is *conscious* that he is conscious.'

"Schumacher calls this power 'self-awareness.' No other animal possesses this rare capability. Yet despite what we may think, few of us actually use it. We choose, instead, the automatic way, the purely pragmatic way of thinking."

"How do we do that?" Jack asked. "How do we develop a state of self-awareness about our life and our work? I mean, when you really think about it, a Manager's Primary Aim is a picture of his life as he wants to live it. It's his purpose, his meaning for being alive. Which sounds fine, but there's something awfully empty about a statement like that.

"When you first brought up this idea, that it is important for a Manager, or anyone for that matter, to know what his Primary Aim is, I thought to myself, 'I've always known that.' That's what I've been doing all of my life. When I went to school, didn't I know what I wanted to be when I graduated? When I graduated, didn't I know what I wanted to do, and where I wanted to do it, and how much I wanted to earn? When I began to think about marriage, didn't I have an idea of what my wife was going to look like, be interested in, and so on?

"So the question of what the E-Myth Manager's Primary Aim was and is seemed pretty transparent to me at first. But every time I try to sum it up now in my life as a Manager, I get stuck. Something implacable stops me. It's as though a wall has been constructed between one part of me and another. The difference between creating external objectives and creating enhanced self-awareness is one of the hardest things I've had to do in my working life."

I realized that for Jack to fully appreciate the difference between the two ways of thinking about one's Primary Aim he was going to have to reconnect with the feeling of being self-aware. "Let's do this," I said to Jack quietly. "Let's start all over again. Let's start by readjusting ourselves to become mindful of the moment."

We each took a deep breath and settled down. As I adjusted the way I was sitting in my chair, I noticed that Jack immediately became more relaxed. His arms were folded loosely in his lap, and he was breathing much more slowly than usual.

"Let's talk some more about the E-Myth Manager's Primary Aim," I said to Jack, who was visibly less agitated. "Okay?"

"Okay."

*   *   *

I began.

"The clear purpose for creating one's Primary Aim is to actively live life, rather than let life live you.

Most people are always on autopilot, so they are completely unaware of the dramatic difference between living and being lived. Only when we consciously choose to begin living again do we notice the difference.

"This ability to be conscious of our consciousness, as Schumacher says, is so extraordinarily powerful, that if developed to its fullest potential it possesses the energy to lift us to a completely new dimension than the one we commonly live in."

"Is that what makes the question 'What do I want?' a *life*-defining question rather than an organization-defining question?" Jack asked.

"That's exactly right," I answered. "Because the question cuts to the quick and focuses us on our humanness. That's why this first aspect of developing our Primary Aim is a universal one. It is to become self-aware. To know ourselves. To discover the truth about ourselves. To see ourselves as we really are. And the more we discover the truth about ourselves, the less likely we will be to subject ourselves to the arbitrariness of the Emperor's Vision. Because the truth has a way of humbling us. The truth is so powerful that we are bound to pursue it in our own way, to realize our own passion and potential in the best way we can.

"The second step in the creation of the E-Myth

Manager's Primary Aim is his commitment to the awareness of other people—to find out what is truly going on in them. Not what we *think* is going on, or what *they* think is going on, but what is *truly* going on."

"But how do we know that?" Jack asked.

"The only way we have of knowing that is to ask. So the second step in the creation of the E-Myth Manager's Primary Aim is a commitment to ask others what is true about them. In a world in which people are not really in touch with the truth about themselves, but only in their *opinions* about themselves, asking such a question will result in an incredibly broad range of untruths to deal with. But knowing that at the outset and not judging it is how the E-Myth Manager can begin to develop a finely tuned ability to see clearly where the truth exists in others and where it doesn't."

"What does this have to do with creating my Primary Aim and that of my enterprise?" Jack asked.

"People are unmanageable, Jack. They're not motivated by others but by their own versions of the universal demons, fear and greed. Yet somehow, for you to create a successful enterprise, to fulfill its Vision and get results, you must try to understand what makes the people who work for you tick. And the best way is the simplest: ask them. Not only does this give you as a Manager some insight into them as human beings, but it gives them some insight into themselves, perhaps even their first glimpse of truth and self-awareness.

"The third step in the creation of your Primary Aim is to try to see yourself as others see you. Few people can truly see themselves as they appear to others; even fewer people understand the impact they have on others. Schumacher includes a brief story in the book I mentioned earlier. It goes like this:

> I once read a story of a man who died and went into the next world where he met numbers of people some of whom he knew and liked and some he knew and disliked. But there was one person there whom he did not know and he could not bear him. Everything he said infuriated and disgusted him— his manner, his habits, his laziness, his insincere way of speaking, his facial expressions—and it seemed to him also that he could see into this man's thoughts and his feelings and all his secrets and, in fact, into all his life. He asked the others who this impossible man was. They answered: "Up here we have very special mirrors which are quite different from those in your world. This man is yourself." Let us suppose, then, that you have to live with a person who is you. Perhaps this is what

the other person has to do. Of course, if you have no self-observation you may actually imagine this would be charming and that if everyone were just like you, the world would indeed be a happy place. There are no limits to vanity and self-conceit. Now in putting yourself into another person's position you are also putting yourself into his point of view, into how he sees you, and hears you, and experiences you in your daily behavior. You are seeing yourself through his eyes.

"Until you can experience the impact you are having on people around you, you can't truly understand who you are. In addition to having self-awareness and empathy for others, you must try to see yourself as others see you, hear yourself as others hear you, experience yourself as others experience you, live and work with yourself as others live with you and work with you. That objectivity will provide you with the distance needed to reinvent your role as a Manager and your relationship to the organization.

"The fourth step in the creation of your Primary Aim is to develop an understanding of the people and processes around you. This is an exercise in becoming intimate with all of the behaviors and operations within your environment, and is a critical component in your education of becoming an E-Myth Manager."

"Why?" asked Jack.

"The ability to see things as they are, as opposed to how we want them to be or are told by others they ought to be, is as crucial to the fulfillment of a Manager's development as any of those that preceded it. For in spite of technological advancement, the information explosion, and our supposedly sophisticated ability to communicate with each other worldwide, we have become more dependent upon these external resources and therefore increasingly more helpless without them. So when these resources fail, and they do with greater and greater frequency, we are powerless. And rather than depend upon the appointed persons within the organization to tell the E-Myth Manager what they want him to believe is the truth, the entrepreneurial Manager must develop a first-hand knowledge of the truth before catastrophe strikes.

"That is why the E-Myth Manager must become passionately interested in knowing and owning the truth of his world. Because until we do, and unless we do, the world within the organization as well as the world at large will overwhelm us and make it increasingly more difficult for us to keep our Primary Aim intact, and front and center. And if that happens, again, our lives will not be truly lived."

"That all makes sense to me," Jack said. "But

when does the actual creation of my Primary Aim take place?"

"That's the fifth and final step in the creation of your Primary Aim, Jack. To compose an impartial description of the life you intend to lead. Imagine yourself as a person who is determinedly self-aware, genuinely interested in what is going on inside other people, intelligently open to the way other people see and experience you, and passionately intent upon understanding the relationships that exist in the world around you. You can imagine that, can't you? Because in many ways, you're already one step closer to becoming that person just by being interested. You've already begun to seek out the truth.

"That's why this fifth step is so critical to developing your Primary Aim. Because it gives you a taste of what it means to become an entrepreneurial Manager. It provides you with the experience of seeing in the moment yourself as you can truly be—intensely focused, intelligently interested, and deeply dedicated to your dream, your enterprise, and everyone you work and live with. Your Primary Aim is your dedication to truly living."

Jack looked at me with great expectation after we'd finished our discussion on Primary Aim. He was clearly excited.

"This is just what I've been needing in my life," he

said with a smile. "Some perspective—something to help me figure out what's really important as far as where I'm going. But I'm not clear on how to reconcile the big picture of my ideal life with working at The Academy."

I laughed. "That'll be the subject of our next reunion, Jack," I said. "You've got a lot to think about right now. But why don't we plan to get together in a few days and talk about the E-Myth Manager's Strategic Objective?"

8

The E-Myth Manager's

Strategic Objective

In martial arts we say, "Put it on the mat," which means to take your philosophy and see what it looks like in action and deed.

Richard Strozzi Heckler, The Anatomy of Change

Three days had passed since my conversation with Jack about the E-Myth Manager's Primary Aim. He was on his way over to my home to talk about the E-Myth Manager's Strategic Objective. The weather had improved; it was a bright, sunny afternoon, and from the windows of my home office I could look out over the beautiful green hills of Sonoma County.

Jack arrived and started talking even before we sat down.

"I've been doing a lot of thinking about our last conversation, and I think I've gotten a handle on what you mean by self-awareness. I'm really interested in seeing how that fits in with what we're going to talk about today. My concern is that being self-aware and building a successful business aren't very compatible."

I was excited to answer Jack's challenging question.

"The first step toward understanding your Strategic Objective is to recall that it is shaped primarily and most indelibly by your Primary Aim. Without a deeply defined Vision of your life, you have no standards by which to evaluate your role as a Manager, no criteria by which to gauge whether the organization you are presently in—or the one to which you are considering going—will work for you.

"On the other hand, no matter how strong your Primary Aim may be, if the organization within which you find yourself doesn't mesh with your picture, you'll never be happy—and you won't be able to do your job well. That's where your Strategic Objective comes in. A Manager's Strategic Objective must marry his Primary Aim with the Strategic Objective of the company, because your role in that enterprise is to create a business that manifests the entrepreneurial Vision of the company. And as an E-Myth Manager, you're accountable for realizing that objective, for manifesting the Emperor's Vision in real life."

Jack looked concerned.

I continued. "The only way to truly evaluate where you are in your career as a Manager is to look at the organization—the work, the time, the money, the people, the product, the ethics, the morality, the culture—and measure it against your own clear definition of who you wish to be. Your desire to become the person you have described in your Primary Aim is what drives you to be conscious, to make choices. Your ability to choose is not only your right, it's your salvation. And if it sounds strange at first, it's because most Managers aren't used to choosing their work consciously.

"The E-Myth Manager's Primary Aim is an intentional personal construct that provides the Manager with an *internal* benchmark against which, it is hoped, all decisions will be made. Therefore, the E-Myth Manager's Strategic Objective provides him with an *external* benchmark by which to evaluate the vehicle through which he pursues his Primary Aim.

In creating your Strategic Objective, you must ask yourself if what you've described in your Primary Aim is truly what you want, is this company, this situation, this relationship going to provide you with the means of achieving it?

"Look at the Emperor. Do you want to forge an alliance with him? Can you? Is he the kind of man you can admire and respect?

"A Manager's Primary Aim can't be his Emperor's. A Manager's Strategic Objective is the company's aim, that is true. And the company's aim is its Strategic Objective. But as a Manager, you owe it to yourself and to the company to consciously choose the right organization, one whose aim serves your aim, one whose alignment matches your purpose, your passion, your design for your own life, whose aim you can fully serve with a clear conscience. This company should be a place where you can grow and experience yourself becoming the person you want to be.

"Can you see why so many Managers are so unhappy in their jobs?" I continued. "Because they have never made the conscious choice to shape their own lives, they have given themselves up to someone else. And because that person was so established, so rich, so connected, so powerful, it was easy to do so. Which is not to say that a Manager should be punished for making that choice—or even a succession of those choices. In fact, it's often necessary to give up your will to another so you can grow into the self-awareness of conscious choice."

At that point Jack interrupted. "That's exactly how I feel," he said. "I mean, I couldn't imagine not coming to The E-Myth Academy when I did, or going through this process of self-awareness back then. I needed your purpose, your Vision, the structure that your agenda provided. All of those things gave me the chance to grow and change, to ready myself for this kind of soul searching. And now I can see what you mean when you say it's crucial that I compare my Primary Aim to yours. It's scary, but this kind of questioning makes things so much clearer."

"That's good," I said to Jack, both proud of his progress and concerned that he might leave The Academy. Who wouldn't be? But I also knew that if he needed to be somewhere else, in the long run it would be best for us both.

I continued. "To fashion your Strategic Objective you must think about *your* ideal organization. If you could invent it, what would it be? What qualities would it have? Think about what kind of an organization would facilitate the development of the kind of person you wish to become.

"Ideally, such an organization would be an intelligent, integrated system rather than a collection of individual 'stores' or people each doing their own thing. This system would be devoted to implementing the enterprise's overarching Vision or purpose, and as a result, the group would be in agreement as to what this purpose was and the type of results it was hoping to achieve. Decisions would be made with this focus in mind. A rational environment would exist in such an organization, as would a balance very much like the balance achieved in a healthy body. Such an organization would make its choices based upon the growing intelligence at the heart of each and every system within the enterprise, along with the information streaming into it from the outside world and from the people within the organization. And just as a body experiences the exuberance that comes from health, so too would this organization experience the exuberance that comes from such intelligence. The clarity of the truth would be the sole driving force in such an organization, because living this truth would be the sole driving force in you as an emerging individual.

"And so, in this intelligent, integrated organization in which truth and knowledge are revered, the pursuit of more intelligence, more understanding, and more exuberance would be the common theme among the people who work there."

It was Jack's turn to talk.

"If the attributes of such an organization are so clear, why then are there so few intelligent organizations like it?"

"Because," I responded, "every day, people as imperfect as you and I flood into organizations, bringing with them their individual needs, hungers, fears, and hopes—some of them conscious, but many of them not. These human systems, otherwise known as personalities, quirks, and preferences, accumulate into a uniquely aggregated person who then goes to work. People are the only part of this grand equation that is unquantifiable. Because organizations are composed of nothing less than imperfect people, organizations are often one of two kinds. I call them conscious organizations or unconscious organizations.

"Conscious organizations are those that possess a clear Vision, manifest that Vision through highly integrated systems, and hold their people accountable for the effective utilization of those systems. Such organizations demonstrate a high sense of purpose, order, integrity, and meaning. And a high sense of satisfaction among the people who work for them.

"Unconscious organizations, on the other hand, are those that are unclear about their Vision, possess few highly integrated systems, reveal little, if any, focus on how those systems are to be used to produce results, create deviously political relationships not only between people, but between people and the work they are expected to do, and generally are experienced as chaos, confusion, disruption, and disorder.

"A conscious organization seeks intelligence.

"An unconscious organization seeks solutions.

"And the purpose of the E-Myth Manager's seven-step process is to help you create a conscious organization in which conscious people can find meaning and success.

*   *   *

"So, Jack," I said, "your Strategic Objective defines clearly what your organization's reality will be when it is finished. Not until the Strategic Objective is formulated will the E-Myth Manager truly own his organization. Does that make sense?"

"Yes," he replied, somewhat hesitantly. "But how do I go about 'owning' my organization?"

"Just as if it were your *own* enterprise, your own business, you must approach this organization with a mind to how it will differentiate itself successfully from all other such organizations. In short, it must distinguish itself as preemptively unique. This is how you reconcile your Primary Aim with that of building a successful business.

"And just as if it were your own business, your

organization must do this for each and every one of your organization's four primary influencers: its customers—we'll talk about those later. Its employees, its suppliers, and its lenders—we'll talk about those too.

"Your four primary influencers are making decisions based upon four categories of preference: their visual preferences, their emotional preferences, their functional preferences, and their financial preferences.

"So your Strategic Objective must clearly define the specific ways your organization will behave under the scrutiny of its four primary influencers— visually, emotionally, functionally, and financially.

"This system of influencers and expectations provides you with a matrix within which to begin the development of your Strategic Objective.

"It asks, How will my organization look? How will my organization feel? How will my organization work? How will my organization justify its existence financially to my customers, to my employees, to my suppliers, to my lenders?

"Your organization could be a sales organization, a financial organization, a distribution center; it could be any function within any enterprise. It could have three employees or three hundred. But whatever it does, and however many people do it, this organization of yours must do it in the context of your Primary Aim, your Strategic Objective, the Vision of the enterprise within which it performs its essential function or functions, and the Vision of each and every Manager and each and every one of their functions in the enterprise of which you are all a part.

"And for each of you, the enterprise included, this same system of influencers and expectations exists as the essential model for creation and implementation of your separate and mutual visions.

"Understanding the E-Myth Manager's mind-set about this is crucial if a conscious organization is to be created.

"That mind-set is this:

"It is not only *your* organization, but all organizations within the totality of the enterprise's organization, that must come to agreement about the matrix it utilizes to invent and reinvent itself. The best way to do that is within your own organization. It's like tossing a stone into a pond—once the stone penetrates the surface, it inspires ripples of movement within the water surrounding it."

*   *   *

"Okay. I've got the entrepreneurial mind-set down, I think," Jack said. "But how do I approach the practical part of my Strategic Objective?"

"Your Strategic Objective describes in as much detail as possible how your organization will look, feel, function, and profit in the minds of your primary influencers," I replied.

"The most effective way to begin this process is to write your 'Company Story.' The following is an example of one such story. Imagine yourself telling this story to a group of prospective employees. They could be customers, employees, suppliers, or lenders. The story doesn't change, since the organization that is the product of the story was created with each of these influencers in mind."

You are standing in a meeting room in a hotel. The audience is seated, waiting for you to address them. You walk to the front of the room, mount the dais. You are impeccably dressed, as if you were going to. an incredibly important event. To the bank to borrow a lot of money. To an investor meeting to convince them of your capability to provide them with a more than reasonable return on their investment. To a wedding of someone who is very important to you. You stand quietly for a moment and survey the people in front of you. You experience the joy of this moment, this opportunity to share with the people in front of you the story of your business, of your creation, of your organization, of a place that has been intentionally created to provide joy for those who come into relationship with it.

You speak:

"*Thank you for coming here today. I am Jack, the director of field operations for The E-Myth Academy. I'm delighted that I have this opportunity to tell you the story of my organization. If we had met a year ago, I'm afraid the story would have been much different. The truth is, I came to a conclusion exactly one year ago that something was missing in my work. And candidly, that something was me. Oh, certainly I worked hard, and my organization seemed productive. But all the same, something critical was missing. I came to the realization that I hadn't made a decision about what I wanted my work, and the place in which I did it, to mean to my life. Once that realization struck me, I decided to do something about it. The first thing I did was to create a picture of the life I wanted to lead. The second thing I did was to create a picture of what my organization needed to look, act, and feel like in order to make my life's picture a reality. Over the past year, my people and I have gone through an incredibly exciting and often difficult process to produce the organization I'm about to describe to you. Is it perfect today? Of course not. But it's on its way.*

"*When we're done here, each of you will get a chance to speak to one of our people about your interests in relationship to our needs. Depending upon how that goes, we'll then take the next step, which will be a personal interview during which you will get to ask all the questions you need to ask, and we will do the same. Eventually, if we both feel that a relationship between us is warranted, we'll make that decision. If not, we'll make that decision too. Whatever the outcome, I hope that you do for yourself what so many of us fail to do. That you will make an honest decision about what you want for your life, what kind of an organization you would like to spend your working hours in, and what the end product of all that time and work and energy should be if you are to realize the life you want. If that happens for each and every one of you, I will have considered this process well worth our time. I trust you will too. So let me tell you about our organization.*

"First and foremost, of course, we are an information organization. But we're not just any information organization. Our commitment goes far beyond that. I would prefer to think of us as a place that facilitates honest and intelligent decisions. Our clients come to us because they have a need. Our job is not to convince them that we can fill that need, but to discover together whether or not one or more of our services can fill that need, and if it can, how, and at what cost. If we come to the conclusion that we can honestly do what's needed, then we design a process through which to justify a buying decision so that no customer has to go through the painful process of discovering, on their own, long after they have spent the money, that our services

weren't the right ones in the first place. When we're done with our process, every client will know, without a shadow of a doubt, that the decision they are being asked to make is the right one. And if it isn't the right one, we'll tell them that before they ever have to tell us.

"At The E-Myth Academy, we call that process 'Our Guarantee.' We call it that because that's exactly what it is, a guarantee that a client will always get exactly what they need, in exactly the way they need it, or we won't do business.

"The process I've just described is not left up to our sales people, it is completely orchestrated from the very beginning to the very end. At The E-Myth Academy, we believe strongly that the system is the solution. We believe strongly that everyone in the organization should be able to produce consistent, highly predictable results. That no one should be left on their own to figure out the solutions to their problems, that the organization holds the first accountability for understanding the best way to achieve any result. And that the organization needs to make the commitment as an organization to discovering the very best methods, processes, and systems for producing results that will make everyone in the organization, and everyone who is depending upon it, extremely successful.

"So it is important for you all to know that we work very hard here to get things done right. And that we are *looking for people for whom cooperation rather than competition is a key indicator of an organization's integrity. Because that's what our people do. They cooperate. With one another. With our clients. With our suppliers. And with the enterprise at large. We are thought of as the guys who cooperate better than anyone else. Which means we're always here to help. Which also means that when anyone walks into our organization from any part of the company, we're up to bat before we're asked. And we do that because, to me, it tells other people that we are absolutely committed to what we do. And we're absolutely committed to what we do, because each and every one of us in the Field Sales Group knows why he or she is here. We know what we are going to get out of it. We know what role our work plays in our lives. We know exactly what we must do, because we have participated in shaping the Group, not just to serve other people on the outside, but to serve all of us on the inside.*

"As a result, the Group looks better than any organization you've ever been in. This suit I'm wearing is no accident. It's part of our code. We dress a certain way because we think a certain way. And the way we think also shapes the way we're all compensated. Everyone in the Group is paid the same base salary. Each and every one in the Group, from administration to sales, works within a formula we've developed over the past year,

which provides every person with an individual Profit Center Analysis of his or her performance. This Analysis is automated, and is pulled up daily by each person for his or her own activity and results.

"That way, every single individual within the Group can determine what they have earned, if anything, above and beyond their base salary. The formula for that calculation is known to everyone, so there's no mystery to it. As a result, every individual within the Group has the ability to affect their own income positively, by looking at what they've done in any one day and by analyzing how they could have improved their performance. Each person then has the opportunity to describe what they learned in a fifteen-minute Snapshot Meeting we hold at the beginning of every day. The Snapshot Meeting is just that. It's a snapshot of what happened the day before, and an opportunity for our people to engage with each other in the process of improving individual and group performance. Everyone shows up at this meeting without fail. It's the juice that starts our day. Of course, there's a system for Snapshot interaction as well. People have to learn how to share what they've learned the day before quickly, so they have to get to the point. Having to get to the point sharpens everyone's communication skills, not only for the Snapshot Meeting, but for all interactions between the people themselves, as well as between their Managers, their *customers, and other people from other organizations within the company. In other words, we learn how to make our point without belaboring it.*

"So let me make my point, without belaboring it. The E-Myth Academy is a place that honors people and process. We believe the world can be an intelligent place, but not if results are left up to chance. We also believe that people cannot create a world any better than themselves. So we provide everyone in our Group with the opportunity to set their own benchmarks, personal and organizational, and then help them in every way we can to realize those benchmarks. Understand, we don't set the benchmarks for our people, they do.

"Which means that the one underlying belief we have, which shapes everything we do, is that each and every one of us must make a personal decision, and then take the responsibility for sharing that decision with everyone else, and taking responsibility for it. That's our motto here at the Group. 'Personal responsibility creates personal freedom.' Thanks for coming and listening."

Jack and I sat for a while without speaking. I could hear the thud, thud, thud of a pitchfork being used with great energy by Roberto, my gardener and handyman, off in the distance. We were getting ready to build a stucco wall around what I call our "meditation garden," and Roberto was beginning to dig the foundation. Later on, Jack and I would join him for a few whacks of our own. Everyone who comes to our home hopefully one time or another gets to contribute something to the evolution of our garden. It's a continuing joy for me to see it unfold.

Jack said, "The idea behind becoming an E-Myth Manager is becoming clearer to me. The connection between people and the organizations they create is almost a spiritual one, in that the invisible, the inner connection between a Manager and himself, and the visible, the outer connection between the Manager and the organization, his people, and the way in which it fulfills its role in the world, must be portrayed clearly, or no one is going to get it.

"So that's what your description of the Strategic Objective means to me. While you didn't talk about how big the organization was going to be, how many sales it was going to make, what products and services it was going to sell, all the while I could begin to experience the *flavor* of the organization you were describing in your story, and I knew it was that flavor that was critical if any of these other more tactical things were to be addressed with any meaning. But having said that, let me ask you a question. Does the Strategic Objective get down to the details, so to speak? Is it important that everyone in the organization know specifically what they are there to accomplish, by when, and how much?"

"Yes," I said, "it is critical that tactical objectives be included in the Strategic Objective. But what is true is that once the 'flavor' of the organization you're creating is communicated clearly, once the standards and character of the organization are shaped with as much clarity as you can muster, the tactical components begin to reveal themselves. Building an organization is just like programming; if this, then that. If this kind of an organization, than that is what we must do to manifest it.

"And that happens, Jack, once the Strategic Objective is written. Once you have sat down to compose it. Once you go through the process of seeing it as clearly as possible. Once you tie your Primary Aim to the organization to which you are going to devote a huge amount of effort and love and commitment. Once all of that flavor is expressed in real words, on real paper, with an honest respect for the real world you intend to create as an organization. Once all of that is done, the details begin to flood out of you almost as in answer to the joyful question you are posing by imagining such an organization coming to life in earnest.

"Do you see what I mean?" I asked him. "Do you see that consciousness and business work not in opposition to each other, but as friends sharing the same commitment? In this case, the commitment is, as you said, a spiritual one; it is the commitment we both share in inventing an organization that feeds our mutual Primary Aims in a way that gives each and every day we go to work in it a new and salutary meaning."

Jack grinned, as he usually did when he was feeling good about the progress we were making. "The real question is," I asked him, "who gets to use the pitchfork first. You or me?"

9

THE E-MYTH MANAGER'S

FINANCIAL STRATEGY

"Our sun is one of 400 billion other stars in the galaxy we call the Milky Way. Astronomers say there are about a hundred billion of such galaxies in the universe, and each of these galaxies consists of about a hundred billion stars."

"You're making me dizzy."

Jostein Gaarder, Sophie's World

Jack and I met at a favorite restaurant of mine in Petaluma to talk about the next step in the E-Myth Manager process. I could see a difference in his demeanor since we'd started talking about creating his Primary Aim and Strategic Objective. By the end of our last meeting, he'd seemed more open, more willing to question, and less afraid of the consequences. That was a good frame of mind for broaching the subject of money.

We started with a wonderful Cabernet and an incredible Caesar salad, and gossiped about things of no consequence for at least half an hour. It wasn't until the pasta arrived that we began to talk earnestly. I started.

"When it comes to money, Jack, most Managers are completely out of touch with reality. Of course, every Manager knows that he is affected by money, both organizationally and personally. But I have worked with enough Managers to know that most are completely out of touch because they think about money in a completely unrealistic way."

"Why?" Jack asked.

"Most Managers have a budget. Every year, they work very hard to get as much as possible for their department or division—their organization—so that they don't have to go back for more. In so doing, the Manager is thinking about money and treating the money as if it were someone else's. And it is. But that's exactly the problem. When the money is someone else's, you don't experience it as your own. Even when I, the founder and chairman of The Academy, spend money it isn't mine really. It's someone else's. It's my allocation, my budget. But it's the enterprise's money. It's from the enterprise's bank. It's from the enterprise's pocket. But in reality, when you get right down to it, it's mine. And it's critical that I understand that at the outset of every decision I make. It's critical that every Manager does.

"Because in a large organization, money is institutional, money is invisible. In a large organization, money is something that shows up on the income statement and the balance sheet. You never really see it or touch it. Not so in a small organization. In a small business, the money doesn't come out of the *organization's* pocket, it comes out of a guy's pocket or a woman's purse. From the rent to a single paper clip.

"This is key to your becoming an entrepreneurial Manager, Jack, particularly because you're accustomed to working in large organizations. You're accustomed to thinking about money is if it were an abstraction. You must understand that money in a small organization is not institutional, it's not an abstraction, it's very, very personal."

"But it's difficult to get your head around that when you're not the boss," Jack said.

"I can understand that," I replied, "but what's true about most organizations, even when you are the boss, is that there is no real money, there is only funny money: the concept of money that no one every really sees, touches, or exchanges. The enterprise feeds the myth of funny money, its accountants feed it, the market feeds it, the shareholders feed it, the board of directors feeds it, and yes, management feeds it. Perhaps most especially, government—the quintessential large organization—feeds it. Take, for example, South Korea. South Korea just received a bailout amounting to $58 billion dollars. At least that's what I read. I never actually *saw* the money, but then again, no one did, not even the people who supposedly lent it. I wonder if South Korea ever actually saw it. It's doubtful.

"The concept of funny money has become so pervasive that even the people who *should* know better, don't. Like the guy driving the brown UPS truck. He's an ordinary guy, just like you and me, involved with an enterprise that's far smaller—and hopefully less bureaucratic—than the U.S. government. Surely you'd think that he knows the difference between money in hand and the idea of money, what I'm calling here funny money.

"But sadly, he doesn't. Why? Because he doesn't really *want* to know the truth. Just like you, Jack. You didn't want to know the truth about yourself when you first came to The E-Myth Academy. You just wanted the job. It didn't bother you then that you were spending your precious days working ever harder to accomplish my objectives rather than your own.

"The guy driving the brown truck believes in funny money in part because it's easier to. It's easier to focus on picking up the packages and delivering the packages than it is to really think about what everything costs—and who's getting paid for it."

Jack looked a little overwhelmed. "So what does this have to do with becoming an E-Myth Manager? What changes?"

"The E-Myth Manager knows that you can't build a successful organization on funny money or with people who believe the myth of funny money. You need to surround yourself with real people who believe in earning and spending real money. Money they've earned, and money they feel a responsibility for.

"To do this you must deal with the way people *think* about money long before you approach how people are going to earn money. This Financial Strategy is a critical function within your organization. You must first make certain within your organization that everyone understands how money works, and how it doesn't.

"And to do that you don't need an accountant or a financial planner. You simply need to engage people to relate to money very personally. From the point of accountability. It's that personal attachment to money that each and every Manager must not only understand, but also come to grips with. When you put in for your annual budget, Jack, and you spend it throughout the year, you must feel it's *your* money you're spending, not mine, not The Academy's. And to do this, you must come to look at money in a very simple way.

*   *   *

"Take the guy in the brown truck, for example. Every day, he picks up packages and delivers packages. He picks up the packages from a brown building somewhere and delivers them to his customers. And he picks up packages from his customers and delivers them to the brown building. And that's about it.

"Throughout the day, he's thinking about lots of different things. Like how many customers will be at home to receive their packages. Or maybe how many they'll send out. Or what his wife is going to make for dinner. Or how his daughter scored on her spelling test. Or whether the rain will ever let up. Or why he has to wear knee socks with his brown shorts."

Jack smiled.

"What he's not thinking about are the direct costs of his daily transactions. He's not thinking about how expensive it is to maintain the truck he drives, or to fuel it, get a tune-up, insure it. He's not thinking about how much his uniform costs, or how much his benefits and his retirement program cost his employer, in addition to his salary. Of course, he thinks about his salary, but only because it's never enough.

"And surely he's not thinking about the less obvious costs, costs that would probably be amortized over all the trucks actively on the road. The cost of advertising, the cost of the guys working in the brown building receiving and stacking the packages, the cost of leasing, heating, and maintaining the building itself, the cost of the airplanes that ship the packages, and so on and so forth.

"The point is, the driver of the brown truck should understand the financial impact of what he does every day in relationship to the profit and loss of the organization. When he does, he will understand what it means to be in the business he is in. And what he and it are actually worth."

"But how does this further his understanding of what it means to own his job?" Jack asked patiently.

"Say the guy in the brown truck now knows what it costs him personally to advertise every day. And he has some modicum of control over that spending decision. Would he do it? Or would he save the money? Or would he spend it some other way?" I answered.

Jack pondered this point.

"To be an E-Myth Manager, you've got to think like an owner, not like a driver, and teach your people to do the same. The only way to get the guy in the brown truck to think like an owner is to get him to understand the financial reality of the brown truck business he's in.

"He's got to become a personal profit center—he's got to analyze the costs of doing business every day and he's got to think about it and discuss it with other brown truck drivers in the organization.

"This is the first part of the E-Myth Manager's Financial Strategy: to encourage every person in your organization to operate as a personal profit center. To involve every single individual in the organization with the subject of money: how it works, where it goes, how much is left, how it's spent, and how much everyone gets at the end of the day.

"The second part of the E-Myth Manager's Financial Strategy is to understand the three kinds of money an organization creates. These three are income, profit, and equity.

"Income is the money that everyone is paid. Profit is what's earned after everyone is paid. And equity is what the business is worth. If the E-Myth Manager owned his business, equity would be the most important, profit would be the second most important, and income would be the third most important. If more Managers were accountable and thought this way, there'd be a lot less funny money floating around.

"Because the E-Myth Manager's Strategic Objective is to become more entrepreneurial and more in control of his own life as a Manager and beyond, equity is a critical strategic indicator of how well his organization is doing.

"This is also true of the driver of the brown truck," I continued. "If he understood the value of his business, then he would have a completely different appreciation for the truck he's driving and the business he does. He'd also have a greater appreciation of his own contribution to the enterprise, and thereby would develop a much greater sense of ownership and pride in his role.

"Of course, I'm aware of all the arguments that can be made to the contrary. That the guy will never own his truck. That the calculation of equity is far more complicated than you could gauge by evaluating any single truck. But what if the guy *could* calculate the value of his business? What if the Manager *could* calculate the value of his organization as if it were independently owned? What if everyone working in an organization *could* calculate their contribution to the success of the organization? What if everyone in every organization *were* so motivated?

Because if they *were*, every organization and every person within them would immediately be changed forever. And the only way in the world that can happen is to teach people how."

* * *

"Profit is the money the organization makes to finance its growth. If the Manager thought of her business as a small-business owner does, then the last thing she would want to do is to go out and borrow money the organization could make. Because the money she borrows is always going to be more expensive than the money she makes.

"Profit is also a key strategic indicator of the successful small business. Not profit for profit's sake, but profit for growth's sake. Because if the value of one's business is measured in the value of its enhanced equity, then the way in which to enhance that equity is to make certain the business grows, and keeps growing, for as long as you own it. The only way to do that is to invest in its growth. And the only way to do that is with capital created for that purpose.

"The best and least expensive way to do that is through the profitability of your organization. Every small-business owner should know that. Unfortunately, very few Managers do. But if a Manager were to behave as though he owns the organization he manages, and treated it as though it were a small business, not only would the organization become more profitable, but the Manager would learn what it takes to actually grow a business that way. And once you learn what it takes to grow that way—and build that capability into your very being—you know that you *can* become the owner of your own enterprise, of your own organization, of your own small business, any time you choose.

"Finally, there's income, the amount of money everyone's paid.

"If there is any subject close to the heart of the driver of the brown truck it's income," I said to Jack, who agreed wholeheartedly. "But if you were to investigate the driver of the brown truck's own financial strategy, his income is never enough. Never enough to prepare him for the future, and never enough for today.

"It is a disconcerting fact in America, that every driver of every brown truck, green truck, lawn mower, pet store, or machine tool, is hopelessly and helplessly caught between a rock and a hard place. The rock is his reality, the hard place is his desire. And he never has enough to feed either."

"Which means he's stuck," Jack chimed in.

"Right. And that brings me to the third part of the E-Myth Manager's Financial Strategy: to teach everyone in the organization about money. About what income is and what it isn't. About how to think about income as if you were the owner as opposed to the driver. And not only how to think about it, but how to do something about it.

"So at the very outset, everyone you bring into your organization, Jack, must be taught how to think about money, how to understand and appreciate their personal relationship to money, and how to see that it is not simply the organization's responsibility to be financially solvent. It is the responsibility of each and every individual within that organization to be financially solvent, and to see the impact that that solvency, that productivity, has on the health of the organization at large.

"*How* you do that, Jack, is not the question. The answers become obvious the minute you realize how important it is *to* do that. The critical thing to understand is that to the degree your people are disconnected from the financial reality of what each and every one of them contributes to, or takes from, the organization every day, they will never be connected to the impact it has personally on them. And to the degree your people are disconnected from their own financial reality, they are not doing the work we described in your Primary Aim. Do you see how all this fits together, Jack? That money is an integral part of the whole? And that until your people and you see it as a part of the whole, you will continue to be disconnected from reality? And that being disconnected from reality is not the stuff of a conscious organization?"

Jack said, "How come nobody has ever talked to me about this before?"

"Good question," I answered. "But rather than trying to answer it now, let's come back to that question after we've had a chance to look at the rest of the E-Myth Manager's strategy for building an entrepreneurial organization. Okay?"

"You're the boss," Jack smiled. "But if you forget, I'll remind you. Because it's an important question to me."

"You got it," I answered.

10

THE E-MYTH MANAGER'S

ORGANIZATIONAL STRATEGY

Truth and change have a powerful similarity. They both deal with a constantly unfinished task. It is the perennial pursuit of this unfinished task to which both the philosopher and the chief executive's inspiration must be directed.

Theodore Levitt, **Marketing for Business Growth**

As a way of opening my discussion with Jack about the E-Myth Manager's Organizational Strategy, I shared with him a conversation I recently had with a Manager in a major international corporation.

"I couldn't believe it," I said. "Here I was talking to

a senior vice president of a major international organization, who was trying to describe to me what the people who reported to him did. He said, '. . . and Murray does this, and he also does that, but when he's in San Francisco, because we don't have anyone there to do this other thing, he does that too, except when he's in Hong Kong—and then everything changes.'

"'Of course,' I thought to myself. 'I understand. That's what got you into trouble in the first place.'

"Because what I was hearing from him was the same as what I hear nearly everywhere I go. Reengineered or not, sophisticated or naive, private or public, most businesses have a completely dysfunctional relationship with the strategy and the idea behind organizing an organization. And that's because, despite their obvious need and wish to get things to work, most organizations I meet are creating conditions that will make it all but certain that nothing works, or if by some chance something does, it does so with the greatest of difficulty.

"And, Jack, I've got to say that it was hard for me to believe at first that, given the investment made, the brainpower available, the consulting, and the amount of money being paid to very experienced people, so many organizations could get this simple thing called organization so wrong.

"I finally came to the conclusion, after many years, that there was something essentially flawed with the way organizations are organized, reorganized, and then reorganized again. And that there was undoubtedly a better way to do it.

"So I developed the E-Myth Manager's Organizational Strategy."

*   *   *

"An E-Myth Manager knows that you do not organize people—you organize work. You do not create a position for Jerry because of Jerry's unique skills, or because Jerry is unhappy doing what he's doing, or because Jerry is your Manager's brother-in-law, or because Jerry has been around for a long time and is getting bored.

"You do not create a position for any person—ever. Not for any reason whatsoever.

"Had this rule been enforced in most of the organizations I have visited over the years, most of the people holding strangely defined positions would be out of work. Tragic, you say? What about the tragedy of keeping people in jobs for which they feel no purpose or passion and which hinder, rather than help, the organization achieve its Vision?

"Identifying positions to which you will assign people requires that the purpose of the position be understood clearly within the context of the highly complex system known as your organization.

"You do not organize work as if it were separate, isolated functions dependent upon the skills of separate, isolated people. You organize work throughout the organization in one fell swoop as a comprehensive system of work, a system that enables the organization to function in the most effective, efficient, and predictable way possible.

"In other words, you don't create the position first, you create the organization's system first, and then the positions will identify themselves.

"An organization must be thought of as one system, not many systems or positions. And the one system must be designed to do the one thing, the most important thing, every organization must do: to make one promise, and keep it!

"An organization must know the one thing it is committed to provide to the people it serves, and focus its entire energy on the perfection of its ability to fulfill that commitment.

"With this in mind, it becomes apparent that the E-Myth Manager's Organizational Strategy not only determines what one's organization does, but how it does it.

"So the first question you must ask in organizing

your work as a Manager, Jack, is, What are we here to accomplish? The answer is the promise.

"The second question you must ask in organizing your work is, If that is my promise, what is the best way to fulfill it? That's your process.

"To become an entrepreneurial Manager, ask, What are the promise and process of my organization? What singularly fascinating result is my organization designed to accomplish, and in what singularly fascinating way does it intend to accomplish it?

"This is the question every Manager must ask, and then answer, in the organization of your enterprise."

*   *   *

"Every E-Myth enterprise is composed of Seven Essential Functions.

"The first three are marketing, management, and money. These are strategic functions. They are the work you do inside of the organization to determine what the organization does outside in the world. They are the focus of Managers at the most strategic level of the organization.

"These functions must ask, and answer, the following questions:

- What is the one result we are here to produce? (marketing—the promise)
- How do we do it? (management—the process)

The Seven Centers of Management Attention

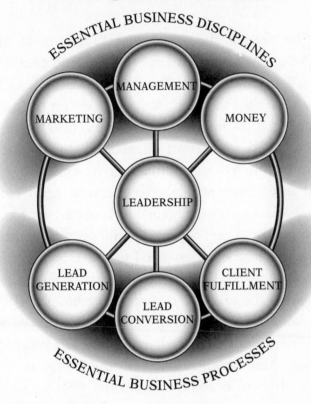

- How much must we charge for doing it? (marketing and money—the pricing strategy)
- How much money will it take to do it? (marketing, money, and management—the capital requirement) and

- How much money will we make when we do it? (marketing, money, and management—the profit and the return on investment)

"The second three essential functions of an E-Myth enterprise are lead generation, lead conversion, and client fulfillment. These are tactical functions. They represent the work Managers do on the outside of the organization to bring business into the organization. Lead generation attracts customers to your organization by communicating its promise in the most direct, powerfully effective way. Lead conversion provides those prospective customers who are attracted by your organization's promise with the rational armament they need to make an affirmative buying decision. Client fulfillment is accountable for delivering the promise the customer bought. If client fulfillment fails to do that, the customer leaves, never to come back again. If client fulfillment succeeds in keeping the organization's promise, the customer stays, often to become a client, purchasing more of what the organization has to offer. Which is obviously the desired effect.

"The seventh essential function of an E-Myth enterprise is that of the CEO. The CEO has the pivotal role in every organization. The CEO is the one who establishes the aim of the organization, makes certain that each and every person within the organization is committed to that aim, and monitors the processes through which his or her Managers do the work of the business they've been entrusted with.

"Every Manager must enter the ritual of management development with one, and only one, role in mind. That role is the function of CEO in an organization of his own. If the beginning Manager's role is that of an apprentice, the CEO's role is that of a master. The trail up that management mountain is the age-old ritual described as apprenticeship, craftsmanship, and mastery. If one is to become an E-Myth Manager, he must be committed to that ritual, or not begin it at all.

"When it comes to the Seven Essential Functions of the E-Myth enterprise, the apprentice Manager is trained to perform and become a master of all the tactical functions of lead generation, lead conversion, and client fulfillment.

"It is critical that the apprentice learn his management skills in the fulfillment of these essential functions, before moving on up to become a craftsman. It is only after having been certified as a successful craftsman, which means that he has mastered all three of the strategic functions of the E-Myth enterprise, that a Manager would be given the opportunity to become the CEO of his own organization.

"Leadership is a rare skill because it requires not

only experience but patience, technical skill, durability, judgment, and a deeply refined character whose sole passion it is to help other Managers achieve a level of perfection that he, the CEO, is still in the process of trying to achieve himself. The CEO knows that by so doing, and only by so doing, it is possible for him to achieve true mastery.

"True mastery is the business of every intelligent organization. There is no other purpose worth pursuing. For without the consciousness that creates mastery, no organization can do more than survive in a relatively flat world."

*   *   *

"I understand that every organization can utilize the Seven Essential Functions to transform the way the organization works and the results it produces," Jack said. "But that strikes me as so theoretical. Can you give me an example of a company that has used this strategy to become more successful?"

"Of course," I replied, delighted.

"Consider a national organization that has a large network of business units, say retail stores. It wants to create a branded image, a personality that is uniquely its own. In asking the question, How must we organize ourselves? it's asking, How can we make certain that these stores do exactly what needs to be done in order to achieve this objective?

"Like most national retail organizations, this organization might decide that the only way to achieve this is to create a network of district and regional Managers. The district Managers would ensure that the stores look, act, and feel the way they should, and would keep close tabs on the store Managers. In addition, the district Managers could also conduct training seminars to increase accountability among store Managers. They could also perform audits on an ongoing basis to assure consistent quality. Are you with me so far?" I asked Jack. He nodded.

"Meanwhile, the regional Managers would, through a series of checks and balances, stay on top of their district Managers, and on occasion may even check on the store Managers themselves. But because the regional Managers must spend time traveling to visit the district Managers, and because there is only so much time in the day, the organization would create a level of divisional Managers, whose primary function it is to check on the regional Managers. All of this, of course, to ensure that the entire system of stores is communicating its unique personality to the outside world. And that doesn't even touch on the layers upon layers of staff and line functions within the organization—like finance, strategic planning, MIS, administration, legal, human resources, and so forth, all of which would be growing like crazy as the new strategy began to take hold.

"Finally, in addition to all of this, in this particular organization there would be a position entitled senior vice president/future watch, inhabited by none other than the chairman's wife, Mona, who has developed a penchant for channeling and taking Vision quests in search of signs that might affect the health and wealth of the organization.

"So as you can see, Jack, this organization has developed quite a healthy overhead, all with a distinct purpose in mind: to serve and protect the corporate body that calls itself Success Stores USA!"

"So what happened?" Jack asked.

"Well, the number of stores grew exponentially in order to keep the chairman's promise to his customers, as described in the motto, 'Because Success is now only a few minutes away!' Which of course meant that they needed many more store employees, and many more store Managers, and many more district Managers and many more regional Managers and many more divisional vice presidents, and countless more support staff, and commensurately more people in each and every management line. And as you can imagine, as the organization grew larger, its effectiveness began to decline precipitously, putting not only the organization's wealth and health in question, but also the essence of its promise. It was clearly time to reorganize Success Stores USA—with the E-Myth Manager Program in mind. And the first thing I instructed them to do was rethink their promise.

"The old promise was: 'Because Success is now only a few minutes away!'

"The new promise they came up with after a lot of soul-searching was: 'Your Success is only seconds away!'"

I looked at Jack for his reaction, and continued with a series of rhetorical questions.

"Haven't we just thrown the chairman and his wife Mona from the frying pan into the fire?

"Haven't we just created a promise impossible to deliver?

"Haven't we just added fuel to the fire of expanded overhead, exponentially more stores, more people, more vice presidents, and more support staff?

Jack looked confused.

"Well, on the face of it we have. But that's where organization development comes in," I continued.

"What we've done instead, Jack, is exactly what we promised to do: reinvent the business using the Seven Essential Functions. The first thing we did was give this giant behemoth some focus. The rest fell into place, primarily as a result of Martina, one very entrepreneurial marketing Manager, who decided to own her own organization—the marketing department—and in so doing, ended up turning the whole organization upside down. With this new focus in mind, Martina concluded, without Mona's assistance, that four trends were coinciding to create an exciting opportunity for Success Stores USA! The trends were: the exponential rise in the number of personal computers in homes throughout the USA; the increased success of catalog sales; the meteoric expansion of the Internet; and the increased interest in and spending on spiritual, financial, and personal development products and services by the wealthier demographics. These high-end customers are also into instant gratification and can't stand to wait a hot second for anything they could have gotten yesterday.

"In response to Martina's proposal, George, the operations Manager said, 'You mean, you're thinking of opening a Web page, inviting customers to it with a catalog, and . . . closing all our stores!? How the hell do you propose to do that?'

"'I thought that was *your* job,' Martina said with a smile. 'But just in case you haven't considered the implications, let me regale you with them. We now have 13,972 people working at Success Stores USA! Of those people, 41.35 percent are Managers and their support staff.

"'For the moment, let's say that 90 percent of those people wouldn't be needed in the new business

I'm describing. Huge savings. If we were to let them all go tomorrow—just kidding—the business as it exists today, without any changes whatsoever, would be immediately profitable. In fact,' Martina continued enthusiastically, 'we could take rare pleasure in knowing that the name of our company—Success Stores USA!—is actually an accurate description of our company, for the very first time!

"'But that's not my point. I'm not suggesting we let everyone go,' Martina said reassuringly. 'What I *am* saying is that if we really begin to focus on our promise and find a way to deliver it unfailingly to our customers, every single time, at low cost, with high impact, at high profit, we could then find a way to organize our people—not only to support that promise, but to provide them with the very same promise: the promise of Success!'

"'How do you propose to do that?' asked Stacy in finance, now deeply interested in the subject at hand. She was rolling up the sleeves of her shirt, and whipping out her laptop.

"'Well, I'm not certain of the numbers. I'm going to need you guys to give me a hand with that. But get the general concept first, and then we'll look at it more closely. Okay?'

George and Stacy both nodded their assent.

"'Okay, this is how I see it,' Martina continued,

taking off her jacket. 'We've got 945 stores. Five warehouses to support them. A distribution center at Corporate to support the five warehouses. And a huge management support staff to monitor, and hopefully control, the stores, invent merchandising programs, marketing programs, purchasing, accounts payable, buyers, technology guys, and so forth. I don't need to belabor the obvious.

"'What if we didn't have most of these people? In fact, what if we didn't have most of those stores? What if we could suddenly get rid of all of the overhead associated with our current business, and still benefit from all of those stores, and those people, but with only a fraction of the cost it presently takes to operate them?'

"Obviously, the answer wasn't going to be offered by George or Stacy. This was Martina's brainchild and she knew it. She went to the white board, picked up a blue marker, and continued.

"'Here's Corporate,' she said as she drew a square at the top of the board, dead center. Inside the box she wrote 'SS-USA!' She then drew a horizontal line an inch below the box, attached the box to it with a short vertical line, and then drew three boxes equally distributed across the board and an inch below the horizontal line, and connected each of them with short vertical lines to the horizontal line above them.

"In the first box on the left, she wrote 'SS!' In the second box in the middle of the board she wrote 'SSD!' And in the third box on the far right she wrote 'SSW&CV!'

"She turned around excitedly to George and Stacy, who were now both sitting down at the conference table peering at the board with growing interest.

"'So, here's the new company,' Martina said. 'On the left'—she pointed to the box on the far left of the board—'we have Success Stores! These are the very same stores we presently have, called Success Stores USA! The only difference is, *we* don't own them, the people who *work* in them do!'

"Martina then pointed to the middle box, labeled 'SSD!' 'In this box we have an organization called Success Stores Direct! This is a group of dealers and distributors who market our Success Stores USA! products and services direct to the consumer as well as the stores. They, in turn, buy the products and services they sell from Success Stores USA! The corporation. In case you're wondering who they are, they're our district Managers, our regional Managers, our divisional vice presidents, and so forth and so on. Who better to distribute and sell our products and services than the people who have been doing that all these years? But now'—she pointed at the box marked SSD—'they're doing it for themselves!'

"'Finally,' Martina went on, 'the pièce de résistance.' She couldn't help but flash her big marketing grin, while she pointed to the box at the extreme right of the board.

"'Here we have the Success Stores USA! Website & Catalog Venture, the entity that brings the entire system of businesses together.

"'Think about it,' Martina continued. 'Every product, every service associated with Success, all available in one hot second from your computer, without leaving your office or your home. At prices that can't be matched by anyone. But not only that. Every store, every direct dealer will be able to input the name and number of any prospective customer, and if that customer buys from the Web site or the catalog, or from a dealer, or from a store—in other words, from any other part of the distribution system, instead of from them—they receive a commission forever!

"'So now we have the best of three worlds. We've got people in stores throughout the country, personally motivated to make those stores a success, because they own them. We've got direct dealers and distributors immediately, completely devoted to selling Success Stores USA! products and services, all of them personally motivated because they own their own business. And we have a Web site into which we're investing the lion's share of our promotional capital to stimulate the consumer to visit us and to benefit from three different noncompeting distribution channels, each of which is highly motivated to provide the best of success to their customers, whether it be through their channel or not, because by so doing they, in turn, receive a commission, no matter who makes the sale!'

"Martina sat down at the conference table with a flushed face and a broad smile. 'I swear to God,' she said, 'I haven't felt this good since I bungee-jumped at a carnival in St. Tropez! Do you get it?' she yelled joyously, looking across at George and Stacy with eyes ablaze. 'Everybody wins!'

"They all sat silently, staring at each other for what seemed to be an eternity. Then, without a signal one to the other, they all stood up with grins as big as all get-out, screamed 'Hah!' and executed a perfect three-way high five!"

*   *   *

"Well, Jack, of course that was only the beginning. But you see that's all it took. Because then there was the getting down to all the questions. How were they going to do the deal to sell off all the stores? How were they going to do the deal to let go all of their people and convert them into dealers and distributors? How were they going to set up their Web site and their catalog business? How much would all that cost? And assuming they could do all that (and of course, they could!) what were the lead generation, lead conversion, and client fulfillment systems for each of the three enterprises to look like? And how would they roll the whole thing out?

"Of course, the answers were really easier than the initial breakthrough. It was the initial breakthrough, taking Success Stores USA! from a doddering old unsuccessful giant to a young enthusiastic healthy kid again that was the trick. But once having pulled it off, the rest was a snap. Provided, of course, that the chairman and Mona bought into it."

Jack said, "I see it now, but I don't understand where the breakthrough came from. Where does the idea of the innovation come from? How does one think about the reinvention of the organization and come up with a conclusion without knowing, in fact, that what you have just thought of is the best way to do it?"

"You don't, Jack. You will never truly know until you go through the process of seeing it, clearly, down to the very smallest question you can think of. And then, the only thing you can do is do it. But you don't throw all care to the winds, you do it prototypically first. You create a new operation, built upon the model I just gave you. You work through it as at the start of a brand new business, which is what it really is. You do exactly what Ray Kroc did at the outset of McDonald's: you go to work *on* your business, rather than *in* it. You build it as though it were the only business you were going to be in; you turnkey every single aspect of it, from the most important things it does to the most trivial, with exactitude, with passion, with a true interest in getting this wonderful new idea off the drawing board into predictable action. As you do it, you begin to experience the truths and the nontruths of it. You watch it intelligently. You originate it as an enterprise, and you do it with true intention and attention, on purpose.

"That's all you *can* do, Jack. That's the way any radical transformation must be done; with intention and attention, by a Manager who has come to his or her senses. And to the degree that the organizational answer you've envisioned serves the life question of more and more people intelligently, only then is it a good idea. And the only way you will know that is through experience."

THE E-MYTH MANAGER'S

MANAGEMENT STRATEGY

The nature of every bureaucracy is to make functionaries and mere cogs in the administrative machinery out of men, and thus to dehumanize them.

Hannah Arendt, **A Report on the Banality of Evil:**
Eichmann in Jerusalem

My next meeting with Jack didn't happen as planned. He was caught up in a project at The Academy that he had to get done by the end of the year, and I was called out of town at the very last moment for a speaking engagement in North Carolina. So as not to lose our momentum, we decided to have our meeting on the E-Myth Manager's Management Strategy electronically. Here's what I wrote:

"Jack, to be a successful Manager in tomorrow's more enlightened, more intelligent, more human, more *conscious* organization is going to be markedly different than it is today. In the more conscious organization, a Manager is less a traditional Manager and more an Entrepreneur. A creator of things. A conductor of an orchestra. An Inventor. A leader. An E-Myth Manager.

"As an E-Myth Manager, you've got a lot to do. But first, you need to come up with a strategy for managing this business. Your Management Strategy is that which enables you to fulfill your promises to yourself, your company, your people, your suppliers, your community, and your customer in the best possible way. It then monitors that process to find ways to sustain, improve, and transform its effectiveness. And the only way to do all of this is through a system. Why a system for management? Because as most, if not all, Managers have experienced but few have understood, there is simply no way in the world to truly manage anything without one.

"You may be wondering if I think it's impossible to manage anything at all without a management system—the answer is yes. Without a management system nothing can be truly managed. Once you realize that, it will become obvious to you that the only thing a Manager can hope to manage with her system is another system. The closest any Manager can come to managing anything at all is to develop a system of processes over which she can exercise control.

"Once you commit to a promise, the E-Myth Manager's job is to manage the process—the system—to keep it, improve it, and rally his troops around it. Your people don't need to be managed, as we've come to know it, if they're right beside you, doing the very thing they're being paid to do, focused on the very same thing you are: fulfilling that promise through the system that's been created to do it.

"What, then, is the role of the Manager if it's not to manage people?

"The role of the Manager is to engage with the present in a fully enlightened manner while inventing the future.

"Take my son Sam, who just turned ten. He's dying to fly his remote control plane. But he can't yet, because he's still in the process of creating it. It sits on his bed unfinished. But, like the life of the Manager who has already committed himself to fulfilling his Strategic Objective, that plane is finished in Sam's mind. Sam is doing what every E-Myth Manager should do. He's keeping his eyes on the prize. However unfinished that plane remains on his bed, it's finished in his mind, and just the idea of it is enough to keep him coming back to it every day. Every day, something gets done. Not everything, but something. Yet, even as the plane sits there on Sam's bed, it is flying. It has been flying in his mind since the day he bought it. That's where flight begins. In the mind.

"But know this: *if there were not passion in Sam's heart, there would be no flight in Sam's mind.* That's what gives the plane its wings. The joy, the sheer unmitigated joy of seeing the thing itself up there, far beyond a little boy's bed, in the world of birds, and clouds, and the soaring blue sky."

*   *   *

"That's the first part of a management system, Jack, innovation. Innovation is the ability to create what could be. Every Manager must do this on an ongoing basis. An entrepreneurial Manager doesn't just solve problems; an E-Myth Manager identifies and seizes opportunities. Problems are endless, as are opportunities. But seizing opportunities always produces exponentially more than solving problems ever will.

"It's also critical to know that attempting to be innovative without a picture in mind of the result you're there to produce is a waste of energy and time. In the case of an entrepreneurial organization, the result is the company's promise, what it intends to become, its Strategic Objective. This Vision guides the innovation.

"For example, Jack, at The E-Myth Academy, our Strategic Objective is to become the preeminent provider of small-business development services and products worldwide. The result of this objective, to transform small businesses worldwide one small-business owner at a time, is the direction to which all of our innovation is aimed. Everything we do, every day, is intended to take us there. Ask yourself, Where are *you* aimed? What is it that *you* intend to do? Is your organization—the way you've set it up, the way you're managing the process—poised to take you there? The answers to these questions should be the guiding light of your innovation and the work every Manager in your organization, or for that matter, in any organization, does every day.

"On the other hand, innovation without quantification—the second component of your Management Strategy—is deadly. Why? Because unless innovation has been quantified, it's possible only to *perceive* rather than really *achieve* a sense of accomplishment. And to quantify innovation, you must be clear about why you're doing what you're doing. You must know for whom and why you're innovating. Because everything you do in your business, everything you manage, produces some sort of result—not just an end result, however, but a series of results along the way. Results that must be understood. You must interpret what the data means in an attempt to recreate it. Having recreated the data through a faithful repetition of that which created it provides you with what I call approximate understanding. But approximate understanding is only a benchmark in the process of achieving true understanding. True understanding comes only when you not only can recreate the data, but know why and how the data was created. The reason for it. The underlying cause of it.

"All of the above ends up as intelligence. All of the above creates one part of the intelligent organization. And as obvious as that may appear, it is remarkable how few organizations come even close to a true understanding of anything they do. Because true understanding is not regarded as a true benefit within most organizations. Indeed, understanding at all, at any level, is normally disregarded in favor of action. The action organization is the one we have all heard described as 'shoot, ready, aim.'

"Intelligence is perceived by most organizations not as I'm defining true intelligence, but as results. In most organizations we are intelligent if we hit the target. We are stupid if we miss. Forget about whether or not we know *how* we managed to hit the target, or in many cases, whether or not we even hit the *right* target; action—shooting—in most organizations is all that's important, despite the fact that they would never admit it.

"In the intelligent organization, these results, which come from the process of quantification, from raw data, to repeatable data, to approximate understanding, to true understanding, to cumulative intelligence, to information, creates a body of relative facts that define the reality of your organization. Understand, it is only that, the reality of your organization. For the reality you create now has a measure to it, a time, a quantity, a set of conditions that you can record, and then recall in relationship to the results of the same process, the same event performed at a later time. And that relationship between one event and another event and a string of events that follow the same action is what I call quantification.

"Quantification—truly knowing the numbers of your business—of your enterprise—and *caring* about them—is critical if innovation is to have any relevance to the day-to-day results you and your people are there to produce.

"Then there's orchestration, the third component of your Management Strategy.

"Orchestration is defined as the organization of work into a replicable system so that the results you *intend* to produce *are* produced, as often as you *wish* to produce them, exactly as you wish them to be.

"Orchestration is the least understood and therefore the least appreciated Management Strategy today, primarily because it flies in the face of the two beliefs that are the product of the information-technology conundrum we find ourselves in:

- That people are our most important asset.
- That time is our most important advantage.

"The E-Myth Manager, on the other hand, believes that process, not people, is what distinguishes great companies. It is critical that you understand what I mean when I say this, Jack. I am not saying that people are unimportant. Quite the contrary. What I *am* saying is that how people produce results must be identified and then repeated if any organization is to leverage itself and the people within it over time. And leverage comes from understanding and developing the processes through which people produce extraordinary results. Why? Because intelligent processes—systems—will produce exponentially greater returns on investment than any one person can. In a *people*-dependent business, the assets go home every night. In a *systems*-dependent business, the assets are there with you no matter who's minding the store. At the same time, orchestration takes the heat off people, because it places the attention instead on the *way* we work rather than *who* does the work. So despite how inhumane the idea of a systems-dependent business might sound at first blush, in fact, a systems-dependent organization is significantly more humane than a people-dependent one. In a *people*-dependent organization, when Fred stops producing, Fred's history! In a *systems*-dependent organization, Fred's never the problem, the *system* is.

"Which is why the E-Myth Manager is continually looking for the process through which results can be produced consistently time after time. Which is to say that orchestration, and an appreciation for the continued leverage it provides ordinary people, is key to building an extraordinarily effective enterprise with a highly differentiated advantage over the competition. Orchestration becomes 'the *way* we do it here,' rather than '*who* does it here.' And any organization that can replicate 'the way we do it here,' in a way that defines its purpose in the world, is truly an intelligent organization. Because to become a truly intelligent organization, it's got to become a brand. To make it become a brand, you've got to develop a way of doing what you do that dramatically differentiates your enterprise, your organization, your business, from every other one. Any organization that can't do that isn't a brand. And any organization that isn't a brand isn't intelligent.

"Let me give you an example of what I mean, Jack, when I speak of the need for innovation, quantification, and orchestration, and the price someone pays for not having them.

"I watched a landscape contractor I had hired move rocks in my yard with a backhoe. Big rocks. The guy was obviously an expert with the backhoe. He loved what he was doing. Yet each time he did it, each time he went to work on a different rock, he dealt with it differently. He used a different technique for each rock. I asked him why, and he responded much as you would expect. That each rock was quite different from the other rocks. Each rock, he said, was unique and therefore required a unique approach.

"The pond we were building was the first of its kind he had ever built. He had built many ponds before it, but this pond was of a shape, depth, and character different from any he had ever created before. Given the location of it on my property, and given the characteristics of it too numerous to mention here, this pond was definitely unique, calling for strategies and techniques that had never been tried before.

"I also asked him why he so often worked alone, by himself, with no help from others. He told me that his job called for an expert, an artist, a skilled artisan with an abundance of experience that could not be replicated by anyone else. He concluded that since he could never find anyone to do things in exactly the same way he did—because no one had the patience, let alone the skill, he had—that he would do every job himself.

"Yet, despite his conviction that every day, every job, and every rock was unique, I couldn't help but notice as I continued to watch him working that there was one specific way he lifted the shovel on the backhoe. There was as well a specific way he moved it from left to right. And there was a specific distance he sat on the backhoe between the seat and the levers he pushed and pulled. He placed himself in exactly that same spot each and every time he used the shovel. And he moved in exactly the same way, over and over again, no matter what location the rock was in, no matter what size the rock was, and no matter how steep the grade.

"While my contractor friend was obviously convinced that nothing he did could be replicated, in fact, a great deal of what he did not only could be, but was being!

"Indeed, it has been my experience that most of

what man does can be replicated, given the intention, the attention, and the intelligent interest.

"Innovation, quantification, and orchestration are the primary accountabilities of the E-Myth Manager, if only so that my contractor friend can expand his area of control to include people less skilled than he, to include more results than he is able to produce on his own, to include more opportunities than those he has limited himself to, and to include more challenges than those with which he has been willing to engage.

"An inability to think like an E-Myth Manager has resulted in my contractor friend doing almost everything that needs to be done himself. It's his habit of mind, thinking like the expert Technician rather than as a true Manager—an E-Myth Manager—that has cost him dearly over time, and will continue to cost him ever more dearly if he fails to change it. Because until he sees that there are opportunities to innovate what he does, to quantify the impact of that innovation, and then to orchestrate it into a system, into a series of processes, that he can teach to people significantly less skilled than he, the job is and will continue to be always dependent upon him. Upon his unique abilities. And by any description, that isn't what the work of a Manager should be. But ask yourself how many Managers are doing it?"

*　　*　　*

"Orchestration, to the knowledge worker, is as foreign—and threatening—as it is to my contractor friend. Because knowledge workers are very possessive of their knowledge. It is, after all, what makes them who they are. It's what gives them their competitive edge in the world. It's what enables them to charge what they charge. Because if anybody could do what they do, it would cease to be knowledge—it would become automation. So knowledge workers— be they physicians, attorneys, programmers, financial advisors, movie directors, cameramen, chiropractors, book makers, graphic designers, or photographers— each and every one of them has spent an inordinate amount of time, money, and interest in cultivating their knowledge, their competitive advantage. And while they have done so, in many cases, for the sheer love of the work they are learning how to do, it is not long before they realize that this knowledge can be sold for a great deal more than it is actually worth!

"So when I say that orchestration, the systems solution to the knowledge advantage, is the only solution to freeing oneself from the enslavement of the expert, I am obviously proposing something that flies in the face of all that knowledge workers deem holy. But think about the price we pay for it!

"Being a one-of-a-kind knowledge worker forces

us to be overly acquisitive, prone to possessiveness, jealous, overworked, and less efficient.

*   *   *

"The E-Myth Manager's management system is, above all, two things: the Work of the Organization, and the Work of the Individual. The Work of the Organization is innovation, quantification, and orchestration. Any Manager who wishes to learn how to do these things can do so immediately. But in my experience with Managers, learning how is the easy part, once you've accepted the validity of *what* to do.

"The second part, the Work of the Individual, goes to the question of the E-Myth Manager's People Strategy (see Chapter 12).

"If a Manager can't manage *anything*, what difference does it make *what* he does? That's a question that goes to the heart of every Manager's true dilemma, the answer to which can be found in your Primary Aim. If you can see yourself as you truly are; see other people as they truly are; see how you are truly seen by other people; see the world around you as it truly is, as opposed to how you think, or would like to think, it is; and finally, if you can create a clear picture of who you would be if you possessed this collective knowledge, you would know the truth. To know anything less than the truth means that you do not possess the ability to do what's true. And if you cannot do what's true, how can you be expected to manage anything?

"The E-Myth Manager's job, as a Manager, is to understand what you know and what you don't, which opens the door to the process of innovation, quantification, and orchestration.

"What do I truly know? then becomes the question every intelligent Manager needs to ask to let go of the past, to engage fully in the present, and to invent the future.

"What do I truly know? is one of those questions that begins everything all over again. It begins the true process of learning. It is at the heart of inquisitiveness, rather than acquisitiveness. It is what Suzuki called 'beginner's mind.' If we as Managers can believe there is a truth in what we do, if we can believe that by seeing ourselves as we are, in seeing others as they are, in seeing ourselves as we're seen by others, and in seeing the world as it really is, we can become more human over time, more conscious over time, more *truthful* over time, then we can believe in the truths that shape our lives and the organizations of which we're a part."

12

THE E-MYTH MANAGER'S

PEOPLE STRATEGY

When we express our true nature, we are human beings. When we do not, we do not know what we are. We are not an animal, because we walk on two legs . . . we may be a ghost; we do not know what to call ourselves. Such a creature does not actually exist.

Shunryu Suzuki, Zen Mind, Beginner's Mind

Talk about management and you immediately begin to talk about people. Why? It's the one thing every company around the globe shares, regardless of industry, size, or profitability. And because every

Manager will admit that people are his biggest problem.

Countless "solutions" to the people problem exist today where the worlds of management, psychology, and alchemy overlap. Open yourself to the possibilities and you will soon find scores of people, each with a different answer, ready and willing to teach you how to engage your people in development programs, create win-win relationships, manage without management, and treat your subordinates as peers. Forget it. None of them work.

The shortfall with these management seminars and programs, no matter how well intentioned they may be, is that they fail to recognize one common, inarguable precept: that people are simply unmanageable.

*   *   *

Jack had stopped by my home on his way to the office for a cup of coffee. Or so he said. Yet I could tell by the look on his face as he came in my front door that something was troubling him.

We sat together in my living room, where a new fire burned in the fireplace. Abruptly, Jack started to speak.

"I've been thinking about the E-Myth Manager Management Strategy. When it comes right down to it, it's really quite ingenious. The concept of managing a system of innovation, quantification, and orchestration really appeals to my practical side," he said with a smile. "But there's another side to it—to me, a nagging inadequacy I'd rather not even mention. And that's got to do with people."

He looked up at me tentatively.

"It's just that no matter how hard I try, how well I plan, or what system I try to introduce—maybe even yours—the sheer irrationality of people always screws it up! I have never in my career been able to figure out how to get people to do what I want."

Jack knew that the next step in the E-Myth Manager process was people development, so his question was well timed. Yet he had deliberately planned to come over first thing in the morning, when he knew he couldn't stay. I sensed this was going to be a bigger issue to work through with him than any of the others. Still, I started. I knew he'd interrupt if the topic got too intense.

"Let's start from square one. People can be many wondrous things—creative, inspiring, and emotional, to name a few. Rational we are not. So when you try to manage someone, Jack, you attempt to enforce intellectual reason upon an irrational organism, creating polarity. In so doing, you create resistance— resistance in the person you're attempting to manage as well as resistance in yourself. Resistance, of course, causes conflict, which in turn evokes exactly the opposite effect you were striving for: an us-versus-them mentality. Anywhere you find this mentality in corporate America, you can be sure that it is the product of well-intentioned Managers who are attempting to manage people. And anywhere you find Managers attempting to manage people, you will find an organization that doesn't work.

"The solution is to avoid managing people at all. And the best way to do this is to manage the system instead."

"The system is what you described in the organizational and management strategies, right?" Jack asked.

"Yes. This system—organized around the organization's common goal, its purpose, its Strategic Objective—engages people in a common cause, rallies them around a collective focus, and diffuses the inevitable destructiveness of an us-versus-them mentality.

"So to really revolutionize the people processes at your company, your primary matter of concern should be for every person in your organization to agree to become a master at

- understanding the system,
- sustaining the system,

- practicing the system,
- improving the system, and
- transforming the system.

"But that's my question," Jack said, glancing quickly at his watch. "How do you create such a system when its components are as unmanageable and unpredictable as you and I?"

"It's a good question, Jack. But it's a complicated one. If you really want to get into this now, I suggest you call your office and let them know you're going to be late."

Much to his apparent dismay, Jack's need to get to the bottom of this "inadequacy" outweighed his distaste for discussing it. I fixed him another cup of coffee and tried to ease him into it gently.

"As a Manager, you obviously can't be oblivious to the human side of the equation. That's not what I mean by managing the system. In every organization, there is a human reality you must confront, no matter *how* systems-oriented you wish to become. Having spent so much time with lots of different types of people in various kinds of organizations, I've developed my own list of strategies people use to get by in their work lives. For our purposes, what I call a human strategy is the position a person takes to protect himself spiritually, psychologically, or physically—something like a defense mechanism. In my experience, I've discovered that each strategy tends to be employed pretty consistently by a particular personality type, so for ease of recognition, that's how I've labeled them. See if you recognize anyone you know.

THE GRUNT

"The Grunt is a cynic who does a day's work for a day's pay. He's not interested in anything else beyond that—not ideas, not Visions, not teamwork, not results. The Grunt *knows* that everyone is out for himself, that the world is a dangerous place in which only the dishonest succeed, and that when anyone succeeds it is *always* at his personal expense. Because the Grunt has already made up his mind that the world—and particularly business—isn't fair, there's no way to win him over."

Jack shifted uncomfortably in his chair.

THE MERCENARY

"The Mercenary is excellent at what he does, and sells himself to the highest bidder. In short, he is loyal to no one other than himself and his expertise. Because he demands a high price, the Mercenary has created an image and a position for himself in the world among the best of the best, which gives him his strong identity and reinforces his value. There is little you can tell the Mercenary to persuade him to your side of an argument. Unless there's some cash on the table.

THE PATRIOT

"The Patriot is a true believer—she believes in causes, companies, charismatic people, ideas, and gives herself up totally to those things. She does so willingly because she has forsaken her belief in herself. The Patriot craves acceptance among a group or cause larger than herself because she has no sense of self. Which makes her a good team player. But easy as it may sound to goad the Patriot into a manageable position, beware. Because she has no internal benchmark against which to evaluate your request, she's likely to ignore it for a more interesting opportunity.

THE STUDENT

"The Student is the Manager's greatest opportunity and greatest obligation. The Student loves to learn, wishes to be taught, wants to know, craves a teacher. For a true Student, any subject is worthy of his or her interest, whether it be the nature of work, or how to set a fence post in the ground. A good Student is as passionate about universal ideas as he is about seemingly inconsequential tasks. No matter how much experience a good Student has had, he will always be willing to become an apprentice, willing to begin the continuous evolution of learning again.

THE INVENTOR

"The Inventor is a continual surprise to everyone around him. He has the ability and the desire to see opportunities where none seem to exist. More important, he is willing to pursue those opportunities to a point where he has either validated them or determined their lack of value. He is able to effectively engage others in his exploits until he has deemed the exploit unworthy, at which point he moves on to richer pastures. Great Inventors often end up leading enterprises, but they can also be found at the very bottom of an organization, battering around a few interesting—but inconsequential—ideas. The Inventor should be nurtured carefully to help him fulfill his potential, accept his gift, and find balance within an organization.

The Nice Guy

"Everyone knows the nice guy. He is eager to please everyone, and to serve no one. The nice guy is always a nice guy until he is asked to do something he doesn't want to do. Rather than put himself in an untenable position, however, the nice guy avoids potential conflicts of this sort by continually keeping himself occupied with the busywork every organization creates. And because the nice guy is so willing to handle this sort of seemingly insignificant work, he seems happy making himself useful until you ask him to do something he doesn't want to do. Suddenly the nice guy turns passive-aggressive, sullen, and uncooperative.

*   *   *

"Do you know any people like these, Jack?"

"Only my entire organization! This is my problem! They're *all* unmanageable!" Jack shouted.

"I'm no psychologist, Jack, but I am a student of human behavior. And given the human condition that we are confronted with every single day of our lives, I have come to the verifiable conclusion that we can't manage people. That's why I propose that you can only manage the system, the process through which people produce results.

"And still, as you say, a Manager's got to do what a Manager's got to do. People have got to be reckoned with. And to attempt to reckon with people without acknowledging that we haven't a *clue* as to what's going on in their highly personalized, highly subjective minds, is just plain silly. That's why when we spoke of your Strategic Objective, we talked about getting to know the people around you by asking them about themselves. I don't expect you'll get the absolute truth, but you will get what they consider to be their own personal truths. And that's a starting point.

"An entrepreneurial Manager begins his relationship with everyone who wishes to join his organization with a great deal of respect and care for them as individuals. An E-Myth Manager selects these people, makes it part of his Strategic Objective to start these people out on the right path, and provides them with the attention they need to fulfill their Primary Aims, while enabling the Manager to fulfill the organization's Strategic Objective.

"But to understand this process fully, we must take a look at two aspects that play a key role in the creation of one's Primary Aim.

THE POWER OF INTERIOR ATTENTION AND EXTERIOR INTENTION

"Every human strategy I've described is mitigated by two significant modifying characteristics, or qualities, of the human condition. I call these characteristics our Level of Interior Attention and our Level of Exterior Intention.

"These are forces that I believe make it possible for the Grunt to ascend beyond his unconsciously developed state of Gruntness in order to discover another more rarefied state called accelerated human consciousness.

"Once he is conscious of his Gruntness—his Level of Interior Attention—the Grunt is able to grow beyond himself, if he so decides—his Level of Exterior Intention.

"To the degree the Grunt is unwilling to do that, uninterested in seeing himself as he is, his world *is* doomed to be as crystallized and static as I described earlier. The point I'm making here, however, is that it doesn't *have* to be.

"In short, a Grunt is only a Grunt to the degree that his attention and intention lie fallow."

Jack cleared his throat. "Uh, excuse me, but—is there a strategy here?"

"Be patient, my friend. I'm getting to it.

"It is the power of our attention and intention that provides us with the innate intelligence to see ourselves as we truly are—and to glimpse how glorious we can truly be. That's the E-Myth Manager's strategy for managing people—providing them with the process, the purpose, the occasion to which to rise, knowing full well that they themselves are the only motivators they'll take seriously.

"Jack, you can try to hire the best in your business away from your competitors. Or you can pick someone who you believe has real leadership potential out of the secretarial pool. But you must accept that neither you nor I has any control whatsoever over who these people are. The top-level guy you hire away from the competition may be part Mercenary, part Inventor, and part Nice Guy. In total, that makes him unproductive and dysfunctional! The people you look to hire should be people who recognize their weaknesses—perhaps even more than their strengths—and truly express the desire to rise above them. People who are this self-aware are generally also willing to assume full responsibility for the role they play within the organization.

"Think of your organization as a school, where each student is assigned a particular task. With this in mind, the organization then becomes a place in which people are dedicated to pursuing their Primary Aims by increasing their awareness of themselves, their awareness of others, their awareness of how they are perceived by others, and their awareness of how the world really works.

"In such an organization, the E-Myth Manager is a teacher. And the work of such a school, of such an organization, is grist for the educational mill."

"When it comes right down to it," Jack interjected, "what you're saying is that what each of us wants for our own life must be clearly understood by each and every one of us—on our own—before we can come to agreement with the organization that employs us?"

"That's exactly right," I answered. "And it's absolutely necessary for fulfilling the organization's Strategic Objective. But having done that, everyone who joins the organization is able to fully apply himself willingly, conscientiously, and freely to the aim of the organization, knowing that in the process each one of them is completely responsible for his own life. Knowing that his relationship with the organization has been made consciously, rather than unconsciously, not only at the very beginning when he first joined it, but continually, every day, as he pursues the

197

Work of the Organization and the Work of the Individual in a focused, intentional, intelligent way.

"The system through which all of this takes place becomes the tradition and the ritual through which the organization is elevated to a much higher level for all who participate in it."

*   *   *

I was a little worried that our discussion about people had either terrified Jack or infuriated him. Judging by the look on his face, it could've gone either way.

"That's all consistent with what we've talked about so far—the individual's Primary Aim, the organization's Strategic Objective, and so forth. And it's helpful to think about managing people in a way that affords them the opportunity to manage themselves," he said. "But let's talk about this system you keep referring to. How can you quantify—or objectify—people who so clearly have individual habits, personalities, and goals?"

"Because people are so subjectively wired, and because our very subjectivity often prevents us from seeing ourselves clearly, the best way I've found to encourage people to grow to a higher level of being is to objectify the organization: provide people with an objective understanding of the organization's goals and your systematic means for achieving it.

"Becoming truly impartial is what enlivens people to reach beyond their means.

"And it's the Work of the Organization to encourage and inspire the Work of the Individual in this way."

THE WORK OF THE ORGANIZATION AND THE WORK OF THE INDIVIDUAL

"As you'll recall, Jack, the work of the enterprise is to create the Vision for the entire organization, and to continually and consistently stay ahead of it. The work of the business—the Manager's work—is to create, monitor, and improve the *systems* through which the Vision is realized. The work of the practice—the Technician's work—is to *implement* the Manager's systems and to provide feedback as to how well they are working in the organization.

"All of that combined describes the Work of the Organization.

"The second part of the organization's strategy is to provide for the Work of the Individual—which is to serve its *people's* most essential needs, the pursuit of each individual's Primary Aim.

"Imagine a conversation between you and a group of thirty-two prospective entry-level employees. They have all responded to a classified ad, but the source of their interest doesn't change the process that follows. They are all expected to begin at the beginning. You start the meeting by saying:

"I want to thank you all for responding to my ad, and for taking the time to meet with me. Unlike the traditional interview, however, I'd like to take some time to provide you with some real insight into who we are, what we do, how we do it, and what that would mean to you if you choose to be here, and if you are chosen. I'm not going to ask you any questions, nor are you going to have to participate in any way at all. This is my opportunity to give you a true impression of what it means when I say it is the heart *of an organization that defines it as either an extraordinary place or an ordinary place to work. Not the products, not the pay scheme, not the benefits, although I believe that if the heart of an organization is rich, everything else within it will be touched by it, including of course, its people.*

"Whether or not our organization feels extraordinary to you is a very individual thing, and a question only you can answer. But it's important for you to hear me when I say that it would be easy for us to provide you with many compelling reasons to believe in us, if only because you are all looking for a job. Most people who are looking for a job have a habit of jumping to positive

conclusions about places where they interview, only to discover that the job they've gotten is either a dead-end street, or worse. That won't happen to you here. In fact, the process we're going to go through together was designed to make certain that you discover what it is you are truly looking for so that you can measure us against your most honest, personal expectations. If we measure up, that's a first step. If we don't, we will have saved you an enormous amount of time and energy.

"Let me describe the heart of our organization as I see it, and when I'm through, you can ask me any questions you wish and I'll do my utmost to answer them for you. Okay?

"I have to say in advance that my organization is not an easy place to work. It's not easy because we place unusual demands on our people. Note, I said unusual *demands, not* unreasonable *demands. There's a difference. Unreasonable demands are those that make your life stressful, difficult, inharmonious, and confusing.*

"Unreasonable demands can be found everywhere you look in the workplace. My wife and I recently had to complete the signing for a construction loan on our home. The meeting was scheduled at the title company for 5:00 P.M. The office was packed when we arrived. Obviously, everyone was busy completing one assignment, one closing, or another. No one looked very happy. In fact, they all looked tired, bedraggled, done in.

I asked the loan officer, Tina, who was helping us with our transaction, 'Do you guys ever close?' Her answer was, 'Well, we all have a life of sorts, but when you're in this kind of business it doesn't seem to matter. Twelve-hour days are a matter of course.'

"I wouldn't want to work in a place like that. I don't think you would either. In a place like that, the focus is on results and only results. In an organization with heart, the focus is also on results, but more specifically the focus is also on people.

"I'm sure every one of you could give me an example of an unreasonable demand. But how about an unusual demand? An unusual demand is something quite different. One of our unusual demands is that we expect every employee to speak the truth. It doesn't matter about what, just that it is the truth as you see it. Now, that might sound funny to say, but let me tell you it is always surprising to me how difficult it is for people to do. Mostly what we learn at work, at home, at school, in our relationships with other people is to do exactly the opposite. That's why I say this could be a difficult place for you to work.

"Another unusual demand we make is that we expect every employee to take full responsibility for himself and his commitments. Some of those commitments are tangible, such as when you say you're going to meet at a particular hour, you're expected to show up on time.

Other commitments are invisible. For example, when you come to a meeting we expect you to be in that meeting fully. Not dreaming, not wandering, not playing with a pencil, not wishing you were elsewhere.

"We're also unusual in that we see ourselves as having two distinctly different functions within our organization. The first function is what we call the Work of the Organization. The second is what we call the Work of the Individual. The Work of the Organization is everything done in the organization to fulfill its commitments: production, sales, lead generation, marketing, finance, and so forth. The business stuff that every organization does. It's how we do all these things that makes the difference between our organization and many others. You might say that when it comes to the Work of the Organization, everyone within our organization—and I mean everyone—is dedicated to discovering what's true about what we do, what works and what doesn't, and why. If it doesn't work, we seek to develop increasingly better ways of doing things, and where we see the opportunity, we work to completely change not only how we do things, but what things we do, so as to more effectively respond to the world we live in.

"To do that well requires a highly honed focus on the systemic point of view. Which means to say that we see our entire organization as one unified highly interde-

pendent system that we are designing every day to become significantly more effective at our jobs. Everyone who works here is taught how to participate fully in this design and implementation process.

"So, to work you must possess an innate interest in not only going to work in your position, but as we say here, going to work on your position. Because very few people who come to us have ever worked in such a way before, we don't expect you to have the skill to know how to do this, but we do expect you to have the desire to learn.

"If you do, then we have a process for teaching you over time how to develop and increasingly enhance that skill. That's one part of what we do here. We engage every employee at every level completely in the evolution of our organization.

"The Work of the Organization provides each and every one of us with an organized process for continually reinventing it. It works, so we don't have to. And by that I mean, the greater part the systems play in enabling us to produce stunning results, the less the tyranny of routine consumes us, the more we are freed to pursue the more meaningful questions of what it means to be a human being.

"And that is where the Work of the Individual comes in.

"The Work of the Individual was inaugurated here

some eighteen years ago, first as an idea, and slowly, and ever more carefully, to the point where we find it has grounded our organization. Nothing we do here is more important to us than the Work of the Individual. Nothing speaks more truly to the question of heart in our organization than this work. No one will start here who doesn't see the crying need to do it, and no one will stay here who isn't personally committed to sustaining his passion for it.

"The Work of the Individual is a fivefold process. First, to become more self-aware; that is, to know the truth about yourself. Second, to become more aware of others; that is, to be interested in what is truly going on in other people. Third, to become aware of the impact you have on others; that is, to see yourself as others see you. Fourth, to become more aware of how the world really works; that is, to truly become interested in the truth of things rather than in your opinions of things. And fifth, to create a very clear Vision of who you would be if you were the person I've just described, and what that would mean not only to your life, but to the lives of the people around you.

"Now, I know that every time I repeat what I've just said to any group of people, a great many of them are thinking, 'What does this have to do with a job? What business do they have messing around with my personal life? What in the world do they care if I'm self-

aware, or interested in the truth, so long as I can produce results for the organization?'

"My answer to those questions is this: people who
are unconscious and not aware of it are of no interest
to us here. And by unconscious, I mean consumed by
their habits. If I am an unconscious person, my personality shapes me, I do not shape my personality. My ego
drives my wants, my wants do not drive my ego. This is
the condition of most people in most organizations
around the world. We choose to do it differently here, to
the degree that we're able, because it makes us happier
and healthier. And because it works.

"Having said all that, let me describe for you the process through which the Work of the Individual is pur-
sued by each and every one of us here.

"There are five essential skills through which the
fivefold process of the Work of the Individual is enabled
in our organization. The five skills are: concentration,
discrimination, organization, innovation, and communication. Concentration is the skill through which we
develop a heightened ability to focus our attention. Discrimination is the ability we need to focus our intention. Organization is the skill through which we convert
chaos into order in everything we do. Innovation is the
skill that turns order into what is called right action.
Innovation is the 'best way' skill. It helps us to see
opportunities, as opposed to problems, and to best take

advantage of them. Communication is the skill that enables us to engage with other people in a way that works.

"The Work of the Individual is assisted by the organization through the systematic training of all of our people in the development of these five skills. When it comes to these skills, everyone who starts here is presumed to be an apprentice. In short, everyone receives the same training. What you do with it is, of course, up to you. Having gone through the process of apprenticeship, one then moves to craftsman. The craftsman moves on to master. The master becomes a trainer of apprentices. And so forth and so on. Everyone who works here goes through that process continuously. We become masters to the degree that we're able to master the five essential skills. And the way we do that is continually being improved, so that no one ever finishes their training. They're just in continuous evolution along with the rest of us at whatever level we each find ourselves at any particular moment.

"Your Manager here has little or nothing to do with this process. Your Manager, in fact, doesn't manage you at all. Your Manager manages the systems you're using, the processes through which you produce or fail to produce results. Your Manager is focused on the improvement, along with each and every one who works with him, of the way we do business here. And because her

focus is always on the process of innovation, quantification, and orchestration, that leaves you to manage yourself. Of course, in order to do that, you need to learn how to manage yourself. We presume also that everyone who starts in our company is an apprentice when it comes to self-management, no matter how much experience you bring with you. So we teach you our self-management system. You're expected to master and use it. It is the same system for everyone, so that at any time you're having difficulty with it, the person next to you can be of help. It is what we call in our organization a universal system—one that brings productivity, creativity, joy, and opportunity to everyone equally.

"That's what makes us unusual. If you're a true seeker, an adventurer of the soul, you'll be right at home. If you're not, I'll bet you're already thinking of looking elsewhere. Thanks for listening; I hope it's been educational. Now let me answer your questions . . . "

When I finished my description, Jack immediately had a question of his own. "You talk about the five essential skills of concentration, discrimination, organization, innovation, and communication. How do you teach someone in your organization those skills without intruding on their sense of privacy? I know I wouldn't look forward to my Manager becoming my personal development consultant."

"Why, Jack? What would bother you about that?"

"I don't know," Jack answered. "It just seems too personal. The job's the job, and personal is personal. Don't most people want to keep it separate?"

"Well, yes and no," I answered. "In my experience, many people do want to keep their work separate from their personal lives, but mostly because they feel put upon. They feel the need to draw the line because they fear that the Work of the Organization will consume them. But if you can show your genuine commitment and interest in people as if they're real and multidimensional, then something very significant changes. It's no longer an us-versus-them mentality; it's about a shared goal, it's about personal investment. You're expressing an interest in them as human beings. You're expressing an interest in their development, their satisfaction, and their success.

"In other words, Jack, if you aren't interested in studying archery, you don't ally yourself with an archery teacher. If you're not interested in developing yourself and your people into truly extraordinary Managers, don't go to work for an E-Myth Manager. Because if you're not invested—if you don't act, think, and feel as if you own your business—no matter how productive you might be, no matter how many sales you produce, no matter how efficiently your organization may seem to run, the E-Myth Manager will know that he's only got half a person there. And to the E-Myth Manager, half a person is like no person at all. Who would you rather have working in your organization, Jack? People who are only committed to the Work of the Organization, or people who are committed to their own work as individuals as well?"

"Well, when you put it like *that*," Jack said, smiling. "There's no doubt about what I would want."

"Well, now you know what you need to do to get it," I said, "And the only thing that will stand in your way is you."

13

THE E-MYTH MANAGER'S

MARKETING STRATEGY

Marketing is not just a business function. It is a consolidating view of the entire business process.

Theodore Levitt, Marketing for Business Growth

I could tell by the look on Jack's face that the discussion we were about to have wasn't high on his priority list. Jack's job was field operations. As far as he was concerned, marketing was somebody else's job. And it was easy to understand why he thought that way. To Jack, and every Manager like him, marketing

211

was something the organization did to attract new customers. But what Jack didn't understand is that marketing is key to how every organization delivers on its promise.

So as we sat down to talk, Jack and I, I knew that I had to start at the very beginning if I was ever going to make the point he needed to hear. Which is exactly what I did.

*　　　*　　　*

"I know you're not terribly excited to talk about the marketing function of becoming an E-Myth Manager, Jack. And I understand why. Marketing is generally looked upon by Managers like yourself as a necessary evil. Ask the Manager of administration, the Manager of production, the Manager of research and development what their Marketing Strategy is, and like you, none of them will know how to answer. Because none of them has ever asked the question before! None of them has ever been taught that marketing is one of those essential skills without which no enterprise can be invented or implemented successfully.

"Up until now, Jack, you've been able to get away with this narrow perspective because you've never had to operate as an owner before. But part of becoming an E-Myth Manager means understanding marketing and its enormous value in creating a successful organization."

Jack got a little defensive. "But why should we? Marketing only attracts more customers. And who, other than the marketing Manager, is interested in attracting more customers? Customers equal work. And we've already got enough to do."

I'd clearly struck a chord.

Jack continued, "I mean, have you consulted the customer service department? They aren't looking for more customers to service. The training department isn't looking for more people to train. And in field operations we've got enough to do, managing the client accounts we already have."

"Look, Jack," I said. "You're right. Most Managers believe they have enough to do without marketing their products or services. That's something other people do for them. And usually those other people aren't really appreciated. That's because to the average Manager, more customers don't just mean more revenue, they mean more commitments and more missed deadlines. More customers mean more disgruntled employees, more conflict, more resistance, and more aggravation. So I can understand why most Managers find the question of marketing to be beside the point. But I intend to show you why it needs to be the whole point and nothing but the point, because everything else we've been talking about here is dependent upon it.

"Until a Manager understands why and how marketing works, and appreciates it for the profoundly important role it plays in the operating reality of the entire organization, she will never truly own that organization. To such a Manager, transformation will remain only a word, never a fact.

"For without marketing no Manager can ever hope to become her own Emperor.

"And until a Manager becomes her own Emperor, the word *Entrepreneur* holds no meaning.

*   *   *

"No matter what an organization has been formed to do—be it a machine shop within a much larger organization, an administration or finance department, a shipping and receiving department—the importance of marketing in its development is paramount. An E-Myth Manager knows that marketing is nothing other than attraction. Did you know that, Jack?"

"No," he replied. "I've never thought about it that way."

"Actually, I think you do. Think back to when you were wooed to your last job. Attraction is the result of a great offer. An offer you couldn't refuse. An offer you can't refuse is the very essence of attraction. And attraction is the essence of great marketing."

"Don't remind me," Jack said, thinking of his last job.

"In short, Jack, marketing isn't what every Manager thinks of when he says the word. It isn't advertising, or direct response, or infomercials, or radio commercials. These are, of course, forms of media through which marketing is transmitted, but they are not marketing itself; just as the commercial is not marketing, nor the advertisement, nor the billboard. Each of these plays a role in marketing, but none of them alone is sufficient to be called marketing. True marketing is much larger than any one of these things.

"True marketing calls for the ability to understand that your entire organization is in fact the product being offered for sale.

"Marketing communicates your promise, it's true, but true marketing has also to do with the way your organization *delivers* its promise.

"So by asking the question, What is the offer our organization needs to make to our customers that they absolutely, positively cannot afford to refuse, *and how do we deliver it*? the Manager is doing the work of the marketer.

"And as you can immediately see, the answer strikes at the very heart of the organization—at everything it does, and how it does it. Marketing is not simply words and pictures and commercials and brochures that are known to be marketing tools—

215

marketing is the entire system through which your organization makes a promise and delivers it.

"In other words, Jack, an E-Myth organization doesn't just *do* marketing, it *is* marketing.

"And that calls for the complete transformation of one's organization so that it can deliver the promise no one can refuse, every single time, without fail.

MEET DR. SANDY, MARKETING MAVEN

"I want to tell you a story about someone just like yourself, a brilliant guy who actually found work he loved, and was in the midst of a very satisfying and successful career. Even he, however, didn't know the value of marketing in an E-Myth–brand business, and he ended up learning the hard way.

"Dr. Sandy Blake owns his own medical practice in Corte Madera, California. He's very successful. On his staff are three administrative people—including an administrative Manager—four medical assistants, two practitioners working on becoming partners, and an office Manager.

"Dr. Sandy, as his people call him, was always busy. From early in the morning, when he made his rounds at Marin General Hospital, until late at night when he saw patients at the office who couldn't get off work to see him during normal practice hours, Dr. Sandy's week was full. Everyone in Dr. Sandy's practice was as busy as they could possibly be. Yet, despite their success, life was difficult for them, because they were always behind. Files were always stacked on the floor, waiting to be filed. Invoices were always waiting to be mailed. Occasionally, the office was in such a state of disarray that Dr. Sandy himself was astonished that the place still ran. And all the while, the practice continued to grow.

"To be a patient at Dr. Sandy's was also an experience. His waiting room was always full; often it was standing room only. In fact, if you came for your appointment on time, you could expect to wait an average of twenty-three minutes before you would be ushered into the examination room by one of Dr. Sandy's medical assistants. But that was only the beginning. In the examination room, one of these medical assistants would ask you to strip down to the essentials, so that she could weigh you, take your temperature, your blood pressure, and so forth, depending on the purpose of the visit.

"Of course, while you were stripping, the medical assistant would leave. And there was no telling how quickly she would return. Indeed, the wait in the examination room could last as long as the wait in the waiting room.

"Finally, Dr. Sandy, or one of his practitioners, would come into the examination room, obviously preoccupied with his busy day, look at your chart, and then, finally, look at you, and ask the inevitable question, So, how's it going?

"This seemingly innocuous question threw more patients than you could ever imagine into a tizzy, particularly since they had already answered it twice before: once, when they phoned for an appointment, and again, when addressed by the medical assistant. In truth, the doctor's ignorance irritated the patients more because of the apparent lack of respect for their time—time spent waiting in the waiting room, time spent chatting with the medical assistant, time spent waiting for the doctor to appear.

"When I became involved with the transformation of Dr. Sandy's practice, I asked patients what their experience with Dr. Sandy had been like. Many told me, with a hint of nostalgia, that when the practice was brand new, and the offices were freshly painted, well lit, and clean, Dr. Sandy and the medical assistants alike made them feel special and well cared for. That was only three and a half years earlier, and already, they agreed, Dr. Sandy was showing the wear. His exuberance, which had been his hallmark, was dimmed. And the only thing that replaced it was the constant hum of activity in which medical assistants and administrative assistants all seemed to have too much to do and too many people to see.

"On Time, Every Time, Exactly as Promised—Or We Pay For It!"

"Dr. Sandy is not an exception. Dr. Sandy is the rule. Dr. Sandy's 'experience' was certainly not intentional, but it was preventable. Fortunately for him, his practice, and his patients, Dr. Sandy realized something very significant before it was too late: if he was to sustain the experience both his patients and his employees had loved so much at the outset of his practice, he had to reinvent the experience so that it could be renewed every day, at will.

"And when Dr. Sandy came to that realization, everything changed.

"When Dr. Sandy came to that realization, he immediately understood the difference between having an experience and creating one. He understood the difference between working on your business and working in your business. He understood the powerful potential of marketing.

"What Dr. Sandy needed to do was to discover at the core of his medical practice a promise that would alter forever his perception of the practice of medicine, his employees' perceptions of the practice of medicine, and his patients' perceptions of the practice of medicine.

"And the promise he discovered was this one: 'On time, every time, exactly as promised. Or we pay for it!'

"Which simply said to his patients, 'We've made a terrible mistake here. We made an appointment with you, and we didn't respect that commitment. As a result, we have compromised the effectiveness of our practice, the joy of our practice, the efficiency of our practice, and the vitality of our practice. We are now committed to changing that. We are committed to meeting you, on time, every time, exactly as promised, or the visit is on us.'

"Of course, no one in Dr. Sandy's medical practice knew how in the world they were going to make that promise, because they hadn't the faintest idea how they were going to keep it!

"No one in any medical practice had ever made such a promise before.

"But Dr. Sandy knew that in the making of this promise he was going to reenergize his practice. He was going to force each and every employee in his organization to really think about the process by which they conducted business—and to find a way to conduct it more responsibly and more efficiently.

"Which meant they had to keep their promise.

"What happened in Dr. Sandy's practice was amazing. Not only did the organization learn to keep its appointments, on time, every time, exactly as promised, but he implemented systems, which he used to teach the staff how to automate the practice, how to clean up the filing system, how to conduct their billing, how to meet with patients in a more joyful way, how to not only keep the facilities in order, but how to make them shine! Because of one promise, suddenly a whole host of new promises were being made, and then kept, that no one had even thought of before.

*   *   *

"So you can see, Jack, marketing is so much more significant than promotion. Marketing done well is a commitment to providing your customer, your people, yourself, with a business experience that is life-sustaining. With an experience of a relationship that is renewing. With an experience of the process of performing any service, or delivering any product, in a manner that says to the customer, 'You matter.' Marketing engages every part of your organization in a dialogue that involves the promise you make and your execution of it. It calls into question the ways in which your system works to deliver on this promise, in a consistently high-quality way that everyone has come to depend upon.

"Understanding and developing a marketing mind-set is a must for every Manager no matter what she does. Because if the E-Myth Manager's accountability to the organization at large is to invent a way to fulfill its Strategic Objective—as we've been saying all along it is—then it is insufficient for her to simply become more efficient at what she does. She must also become stunningly more effective in a way that differentiates her organization from the competition.

"No organization can expect to be thought of as a world-class performer if the organizations within it fail to achieve consistently high levels of performance; the system is only as good as the components within it.

"So the question every E-Myth Manager must ask is, What would world-class performance in an organization such as mine look like, feel like, act like, perform like?

"And the only way that question can be answered effectively is to know who the organization is attempting to serve and what they want. Or, in the case of Dr. Sandy, what don't they want! Find out what's keeping them awake at night and how your organization can promise to solve that problem.

"What Dr. Sandy did was to look at the key frustrations of his patients first, and his people second, and come to a very obvious conclusion: waiting pissed people off! Not only the people who were being forced to wait, but the people who were forcing them to wait. They too felt powerless as a result of the office's inefficiencies.

"The truth is that every manger has a 'waiting room' if she only knew where to look, and was interested in looking for it.

"To become an E-Myth Manager, you must always ask the question, Where is my waiting room? What's driving my customers crazy? What's my version of 'On time, every time, exactly as promised'? And what would happen to my business if I could actually make that promise, and then keep it?

"So, Jack, I hope I've made my point. What's *your* waiting room at The Academy? What's driving *your* customers nuts? How many ways are you and your people making it difficult for the people you affect on a day-to-day basis to get the results they're being held accountable for, and how could you make their lives so much easier? And once you discover the answers to those questions, how quickly can you do it? Today, tomorrow, the next day? The answers to these questions aren't about solving problems, they're about seizing opportunities. When you treat the organization as if you own it, you become accountable for every system and strategy that runs it, and that includes marketing. As an E-Myth Manager, you make your own success. And once you've made it, make it again."

EPILOGUE

Jack and I have finished our conversation—for now.

Not that we are done, not by a long shot. But the essential conversation was completed. The *what* of it. And as I said early on in this dialogue of ours, the *what* of it is really the crux of it all.

Jack took that well, although most Managers don't. Most Managers want to jump to the *how* of it, to cut to the bottom line, so to speak. That's because most Managers aren't Managers at all, but Technicians suffering from a management seizure, so accustomed are they to doing it, doing it, doing it.

Perhaps you have a feeling for what this means to you, this focus on getting the job done, this intense need most Managers have for cutting through the impasse they experience in their people by simply doing the job themselves.

If I've done my job, you now understand that there is only one way to cut through the impasse, and that is to stop trying to get results in the ways you have been taught. You can't get there from here. No, the only way you can get results through your people is to reinvest some energy in creating a new relationship with yourself.

Jack came to see me several weeks after our last conversation. He looked like a different man. His face was softer than I had remembered, his hard-edged intensity gone. He smiled at me warmly and asked if we could talk for just a bit. I nodded, and he began.

He told me that his wife and he had spent more time together in the past three weeks than they had the entire year before. "Talking about things," as Jack put it. "We talked about what it felt like at the beginning of our relationship, how much in love we were. And how, over the past few years, it felt like the bottom had fallen out. I had my stuff to do, and she had hers. Somehow, nothing connected. We were like two strangers walking down parallel paths, never touching, never engaging. Never loving anymore. Then, in the middle of our conversation, Michael, something extraordinary happened. I saw her face for the first time in years. I saw a completely different person than any I had ever seen before. I saw this beautiful complex shift in her eyes, as though I was looking into her very soul. And I fell in love with her all over again. But not like any love I had ever felt before. I couldn't explain it, but we simply sat there, looking into each other's eyes, holding hands, and sobbing. The two of us, sitting there, coming to the realization that we had just been given a second chance.

"And do you know what it was, Michael, this second chance? It was that I had reconnected with myself all over again. What I realized is that we were disconnected from each other because I had been disconnected from myself. And because now I had come into contact with myself, there was suddenly someone home, a real person wanting to be—and able to be—in a relationship as opposed to alone. The process of self-discovery that I've engaged in in becoming an E-Myth Manager has brought my life into focus for the first time in years.

"I know this must sound strange to you," Jack went on, gaining momentum, "but to be alone, to be trapped in the idea of a job or a career, to be caught up in the useless activity and chatter that I had given myself up to over all these years, almost cost me everything I had ever valued in my life. As a student, I was constantly learning, growing, and loving the questions, as opposed to the answers. And now I feel like that's a part of my life again, and I'm a better Manager as a result of it."

Jack settled back in the chair he was sitting in. I

knew the feeling he was talking about. I knew what it felt like to lose a part of yourself, and then, for no understandable reason, to discover it again, as young as it had always been, as fresh and as active as if it had never gone. I could feel what was going on in Jack, as if it were going on in me. In that moment, I knew him. As certainly as I knew me.

"Jack," I said, "the ability that we have to be open and conscious in our lives and in our work, is such a stunning experience. To be vulnerable, to be interested, to be awake, to be challenged, and to feel that the challenge is not in opposition to you, but a part of your being. That's what I felt as you just talked to me. I felt your willingness to share something with me you would have never shared with yourself before, let alone with me, a stranger, a guy you hardly know. And I was touched by it. Thank you for including me in your experience."

*   *   *

And isn't that the only reason for our being together here, dear reader? If you've come this far, it is because there was something missing from your life and work, something you wanted to rediscover before it was too late? And isn't that something, you?

The E-Myth Manager is the better part of everyone, waiting to explore uncharted territory, waiting to discover what it means to be alive. Waiting to discover, like Jack, the experience of truly being first a human being, and then a Manager.

Thank you for sharing your time with me. If you care to, tell me what happens once this sinks in. And I'll tell you what happens to me.

About the Author

MICHAEL GERBER is a small-business revolutionary who has been successfully bringing his E-Myth-Brand Revolution to the dramatic improvement of world-wide small business for the past two decades. Michael Gerber travels around the world addressing hundreds of thousands of small, mid-size, and very large organization managers and owners with his compellingly original message; a message that his clients say has transformed their lives. Over the past twenty years, Mr. Gerber's E-Myth Academy has provided his E-Myth Mastery Program to more than 15,000 small and large organizations, making The E-Myth Academy the largest small-business consulting firm of its kind. His books, audiotapes, and videotape programs continue to be among the top sellers in every category throughout the world—a testament to the fact that Michael Gerber strikes a resonant chord in everyone who wishes to become more effective in their lives.